THE LEGAL
BLOGGING
FOR LAWYERS

RUTH CARTER

ABALAW
PRACTICE
DIVISION
The Business of Practicing Law

Commitment to Quality: The Law Practice Division is committed to quality in our publications. Our authors are experienced practitioners in their fields. Prior to publication, the contents of all our books are rigorously reviewed by experts to ensure the highest quality product and presentation. Because we are committed to serving our readers' needs, we welcome your feedback on how we can improve future editions of this book.

Cover design by RIPE Creative, Inc.

Nothing contained in this book is to be considered as the rendering of legal advice for specific cases, and readers are responsible for obtaining such advice from their own legal counsel. This book and any forms and agreements herein are intended for educational and informational purposes only.

The products and services mentioned in this publication are under trademark or service-mark protection. Product and service names and terms are used throughout only in an editorial fashion, to the benefit of the product manufacturer or service provider, with no intention of infringement. Use of a product or service name or term in this publication should not be regarded as affecting the validity of any trademark or service mark.

The Law Practice Division of the American Bar Association offers an educational program for lawyers in practice. Books and other materials are published in furtherance of that program. Authors and editors of publications may express their own legal interpretations and opinions, which are not necessarily those of either the American Bar Association or the Law Practice Division unless adopted pursuant to the bylaws of the Association. The opinions expressed do not reflect in any way a position of the Division or the American Bar Association, nor do the positions of the Division or the American Bar Association necessarily reflect the opinions of the author.

Printed in the United States of America.

Library of Congress Cataloging-in-Publication Data

Carter, Ruth (Lawyer)
 The legal side of blogging for lawyers / Ruth Carter.
   pages cm. --
 Includes index.
 ISBN 978-1-61438-954-5
 1. Blogs--Law and legislation--United States. 2. Lawyers--United States--Blogs. I. Title.
 KF320.I57C37 2014
 343.7309'99--dc23

                                                                    2013050264

Discounts are available for books ordered in bulk. Special consideration is given to state bars, CLE programs, and other bar-related organizations. Inquire at Book Publishing, American Bar Association, 321 North Clark Street, Chicago, Illinois 60654-7598.

www.ShopABA.org

Dedication

For my fellow legal eagles who constantly remind everyone that there's more than one way to be a lawyer by ignoring the box and breaking the mold.

Contents

About the Author .... *xi*

Acknowledgments .... *xiii*

Disclaimer .... *xv*

Introduction   The Undeniable Ruth   **1**

My Rule of Thumb 3

Chapter 1   Blogging and the First Amendment   **5**

The Right to be Anonymous 6

Not All Speech Is Protected 8

The Difference Between Fact and Opinion 11

Chapter 2   Copyright Basics   **15**

Copyright Rights 16

What is a Derivative Work? 17

Automatic Copyright Protection 18

Copyright Applies to Expression, Not Ideas or Facts 19

Transferring a Copyright 21

Releasing Your Work into the Public Domain 23

Chapter 3   Integrating Others' Work into Your Blog   25

Fair Use..25

Creative Commons Images...30

When In Doubt, Ask Permission...31

Chapter 4   Copyright Registration   33

How to Register Your Blog..33

Blogs Are Not Serial Works...35

Blogs Might Be Derivative Works..36

When Is a Blog Published?..36

Should You Register Your Blog Copyrights? 37

Registering a Blog Written Anonymously or Pseudonymously..........40

Chapter 5   Protecting Your Copyright   43

Policing the Internet for Copyright Infringement........................44

Digital Millennium Copyright Act...45

If Someone Sends a DMCA Takedown Notice to Your Web Host.....48

Should You Register a DMCA Agent?.....................................50

Be Aware of DMCA Abuse...51

Chapter 6   Blogging for Others   53

Blogging as an Employee..54

Independent Contractors..55

Are You an Employee or an Independent Contractor?...................57

Licensing Your Blog Content 58

Chapter 7   Protecting Confidential Sources   61

**Chapter 8   Legal Risks with Allowing Comments and
Guest Posts on Your Blog   65**

Responding to Blog Comments 66

Benefits of Blog Comments...66

Legal Risks Related to Blog Comments....................................67

Consider Creating Terms of Service for Your Blog 68

Legal Risks with Guest Posts on Your Blog 69

Create a Work Made for Hire Contract 69

Indemnify Yourself. 70

Other Contract Provisions. 71

Register a DMCA Agent with the Copyright Office 72

Alternative to Guest Posts 73

Chapter 9   Defamation   75

Defamation Cases Involving Anonymous Persons. 78

Public vs. Private Persons 80

Defamation of a Public Person 80

Defamation of a Private Person. 81

Defamation Defenses. 82

Defense 1: The statement was true. 83

Defense 2: The statement was "substantially true." 83

Defense 3: No one would believe that the statement in question
was asserting a fact. 84

Defense 4: There was no malice. 84

Defense 5: There was no reputational damage. 85

Chapter 10   Invasion of Privacy and Intentional Infliction of Emotional Distress   87

Invasion of Privacy— False Light 88

Invasion of Privacy—Public Disclosure of Private Facts 90

Invasion of Privacy—Intrusion into Seclusion 90

Invasion of Privacy—Misappropriation or Commercialization. 91

Intentional Infliction of Emotional Distress. 92

Chapter 11   Blogging and Trademark Law   95

What's a Trademark? 95

Scope of Trademark Protection 96

What's the Difference Between TM and ®?. 99

How to Register a Trademark 99

Trademark Problems Related to Blogs. 100

Chapter 12   Jurisdictional Issues   **105**

Personal Jurisdiction... 105

Subject Matter Jurisdiction 106

Which State Law Applies?.. 107

Chapter 13   Getting Fired Because of Your Blog   **111**

National Labor Relations Act 112

What You Can Blog About Without Being Fired...................... 114

How Your Blog Can Get You Fired 116

This Is a Gray Area 117

Chapter 14   Getting Arrested Because of Your Blog   **119**

Threats of Violence 119

Threats Against the President of the United States.................... 120

Cyberharassment 121

Illegal Sales 122

Solicitation 122

Chapter 15   Death by Blogging   **125**

Chapter 16   Benefits of Being a Legal Blogger   **129**

Establish Expertise and Build Credibility.............................. 130

Leverage Your Blog for Other Opportunities.......................... 131

Show Your Personality 133

Build Relationships Through Conversations 135

Blogging Is a Commitment.. 136

The Risk of Giving It Away for Free 137

Chapter 17   Ethical Issues with Having a Legal Blog   **141**

Does a Legal Blog Constitute Advertising?............................. 142

Avoiding Solicitation 144

Disclaimers.. 145

Blogging about Your Cases.. 148

Responding to Requests for Advice 149

Disclosing Relationships When You Get
    Free Merchandise and Opportunities 150
Legal Issues Related to Testimonials from Clients and
    Peer Recommendations.. 152
Paid Links 152
Compliance and Penalties for Violating This Rule..................... 153

Chapter 18   Promoting Your Blog   **157**

Be Mindful of Your Ethical Rules 157
Write Quality Content... 158
Create an Action Plan to Promote Your Blog 159
Make Yourself Easy to Find with Keywords............................ 160
Go to Your Readers.. 161
Interact and Be Responsive 163
Be Controversial 164
Use Your Network.. 165
Guest Blogging for Others 166
Take Your Interactions into the Real World........................... 166
Be Patient but Persistent 167

Chapter 19   Final Thoughts   **169**

How to Grow a Thick Skin 170
Be Authentic 171
Be Bold 171

Afterword   From the Blogging Trenches—The Namby Pamby   **173**

Appendix A   State and Federal Laws Related to Blogging   **177**

Appendix B   Online Resources Related to Blogging   **201**

Appendix C   Additional Books on Blogging and Social
    Media Marketing   **203**

Index   **205**

About the Author

Known for her outgoing personality and daring antics, Ruth Carter is the owner of Carter Law Firm in Phoenix, Arizona. Her practice focuses on business formation and contracts, intellectual property, social media law, and flash mob law. When she's not busy being a lawyer, Ruth volunteers with Ignite Phoenix—an event that allows speakers to share their passions with the most engaging audience in the Phoenix metro area. She was selected as an American Bar Association Legal Rebel for her work in flash mob law in 2012 and was named one of the *Phoenix Business Journal's* 40 Under 40 in 2013.

Ruth has been blogging since 2009. She blogs every week on her law firm's site[1] and on her personal blog, *The Undeniable Ruth*.[2] She garnered national attention in the legal community when she leveraged her

---

1. Carter Law Firm blog, last visited October 29, 2013, http://carterlawaz.com/blog.
2. *The Undeniable Ruth*, last visited October 29, 2013, http://www.undeniableruth.com.

blog to pay for part of her law school tuition through her Sponsor A Law Kid program.[3] Ruth also blogs for *Attorney at Work* and *Law.com*.

Ruth lives in Phoenix, Arizona, with her basset hound, Rosie.

You can contact Ruth at Ruth@CarterLawAZ.com.

3.   Sponsor A Law Kid, *The Undeniable Ruth*, last visited October 29, 2013, http://undeniableruth. com/sponsor-a-law-kid.

Acknowledgments

To say that my writing schedule this year has been hectic would be an understatement. I don't recommend writing two books in a nine-month period. There are quite a few people who I need to thank for making this book possible and keeping me sane in the process.

To the wonderful publishing team at the ABA Law Practice Division, especially my project manager Shawn L. Holahan, thank you for making this demanding process as doable and easy as possible. Your support and guidance have been invaluable.

To the Electronic Frontier Foundation in San Francisco, my hat is off to you. Thank you for your tireless efforts to protect and advocate for bloggers' rights. You inspire me.

To my friends Jeff Moriarty and Evo Terra who constantly remind me what it means to show up for your life. Jeff—you are my partner-in-crime, my sounding board when I have writers' block, and a friend for the journey. When you go after your dreams despite fears and adversity, it motivates me to do the same. Evo—you are my role model when it comes to speaking my mind and being myself without asking for permission or forgiveness. When I face adversity, I can always count on you to remind me to say "f**k 'em" and do what I need to do.

To my fellow social media, intellectual property, and First Amendment lawyer friends who always take my calls, I love batting around ideas with you. We're still figuring out how the old laws apply to new technologies and what new laws we need to write. Hopefully, we get it right the first time so we don't have to go back and fix it later.

To everyone who told me to start a blog in 2009, thank you for telling me that I have a voice and a perspective worth sharing. Because of you, I started the blog that led to a professional writing career. Thanks for your faith in me.

To my fellow bloggers (legal and otherwise) who inspire greatness and constantly lead by example, I am so grateful that you share your amazing ideas and insights with the online community and show the rest of us how to do this blogging thing right.

To all my readers, thank you for your love and support, especially those of you who have stuck with me since my early days as a blogger. I am nothing without you. I hope to give you something worth reading every week for a long time.

To my family and friends who encourage my insane ideas and crazy dreams, it's been an easier journey knowing that you have my back.

And last, but certainly not least, to my beloved dog Rosie who lays at my feet, thank you for reminding me how important it is to step away from my computer from time to time and go out to play.

Disclaimer

This book discusses numerous legal issues related to blogging.

- While I am a lawyer, I am not your lawyer.
- Reading this book does not create a lawyer-client relationship between us.
- If you need legal advice regarding your blog, please hire a licensed lawyer in your community.
- This book should only be used as general information.
- It does not constitute legal advice.

Introduction
THE UNDENIABLE RUTH

I started blogging because I was told I have a unique voice and a perspective worth sharing. I could say anything I wanted and no one could stop me![1] The idea of having my own digital soapbox was empowering and validating, though I'll admit I was apprehensive about the commitment and the potential repercussions. But these fears weren't enough to dissuade me.

I've known I was a good writer since I was required to take an expository writing class in high school. That's where I began to learn to let go of traditional essay formats and just let the thoughts flow as if I were speaking. I learned that words in nonfiction writing have a profound impact that was different than anything I'd experienced in any literature course. I rarely remember much when I read fictional works because they're not real and—most of the time—not worth taking up space in my head. When a writer speaks the truth, it sticks with me. And when I speak the truth, I see the impact on others.

---

1. Well, you can't stop me as long as I don't do anything wrong.

1

During law school, I became active on social media, particularly Facebook and Twitter.[2] Many of my friends outside of law school were involved in social media marketing, podcasting, and blogging, and they encouraged me to become more involved. I loved the interactions and reading people share what was important to them.

I started my personal blog, *The Undeniable Ruth*, in January 2010.[3] Early on, I was happy to get double-digit readership on any day, and I was ecstatic to get a comment on a post. At first I struggled to figure out what I wanted to say in my posts each week. It felt awkward, like I was talking to an abyss, not knowing if anyone could hear me. Over time I developed a strong sense of ownership. This was my forum, my chance to express myself, and it didn't really matter if anyone heard me. There were things that needed to be said. Don't get me wrong, it's wonderful to see that people are reading and enjoying my work; but I've learned to say what's on my mind and not necessarily what my readers say they want to hear.

As a blogger, I continue to write the way I speak. I'm not always kind. I have a need to share the truth. I call a spade a spade, and people thank me for having the courage to say what they were thinking. They find it validating.

Early on in my blogging career, I heard a journalist's motto that I've since adopted too: "Comfort the afflicted, and afflict the comfortable." Sometimes I wonder why I choose to be a voice for others who may not be able to speak for themselves, which in turn makes me a target for ridicule. But there are things that need to be said. And if I don't say them, then who will?

I am grateful for the opportunity to be that voice. I think most bloggers accept that not everyone is going to like what we have to say, but that doesn't mean they can stop us from speaking.

---

2.   I don't let people who I don't know in real life connect with my personal Facebook page, but please connect with me on Twitter: http://www.twitter.com/rbcarter.

3.   *The Undeniable Ruth*, last visited October 29, 2013, http://undeniableruth.com.

However, this opportunity also comes with the obligation of keeping ourselves out of trouble. I found myself asking questions like:

How much can I say without getting into trouble?

How can I call someone out?

How do I respond to comments?

Do I need to worry about being fired for saying what I want to say?[4]

I started doing research into the dos and don'ts of blogging and the various ways the law protects those who choose to step up to the digital microphone despite the risk of backlash. My research turned into blog posts, which turned into a paper for my Cyberlaw class, which turned into an e-book for non-lawyer bloggers, and now there's this book for you.

When I opened Carter Law Firm in 2012, I knew that meant I was starting a second blog.[5] Creating my website was a top priority once the required business infrastructure was in place. In a way, having two blogs has been an asset. It gives me twice as many opportunities to share my thoughts every week. My readers can choose to follow either or both blogs depending on their needs, and since each blog is more targeted now, the readership for both sites has grown.

I'm sure some people find blogging intimidating and feel that taking the time to do it is a chore, but I absolutely love it. I couldn't imagine my life without blogging.

MY RULE OF THUMB

One thing you should always remember about online communication is that it is permanent. Even if you remove a post, there will always be a record of its existence on a server somewhere. If you

---

4.   I'm pretty sure my law school blogging made me essentially unemployable in conservative Arizona.

5.   Carter Law Firm blog, last visited October 29, 2013 http://carterlawaz.com/blog.

post anonymously, there will always be a digital trail back to at least the IP address where you created the post.

My general rule of thumb for staying out of trouble is, "Don't post anything on the Internet that you wouldn't put on the front page of the newspaper." When you post a new entry to a blog, you need to act as if your boss, best friend, worst enemy, spouse, and your mother are going to read it. If you have a problem with any of these people seeing a post, you shouldn't publish it. There's still a chance that you'll do something that will get you into trouble, but following this rule decreases the likelihood of that happening.

Chapter 1

BLOGGING AND THE FIRST AMENDMENT

Many lawyers and other legal professionals (myself included) started blogging because we wanted a forum for sharing our thoughts and feelings. You might have fiery opinions or a unique perspective on the law, or life in general. Thankfully, the First Amendment protects the majority of what most people want to say in their blogs, including unpopular or controversial stances on issues. Blogs provide valuable outlets for discussing the issues and ideas that are most important to us.

The First Amendment protects the freedom of speech.[6] This law supports the notion that "debate on public issues should be uninhibited, robust, and wide-open."[7] In many cases, it even protects caustic and sharp attacks. We are lucky to live in the United States, where we are expected to question tradition, authority, and our leaders.

---

6. U.S. Constitution, Amend. I.
7. Currier v. Western Newspapers, Inc., 855 P.2d 1351, 1354 (Ariz. 1993), quoting New York Times Co. v. Sullivan, 376 U.S. 254, 270 (1964).

Freedom of speech applies to written and verbal speech, as well as speech on the Internet.[8] If it is legal to publish something in a book, newspaper, or journal, it is generally permissible to publish it online. This includes your blog, social media websites, and comments you leave on other people's blogs and other Internet forums. Different websites may have additional rules about what is and is not permissible to post.

THE RIGHT TO BE ANONYMOUS

The First Amendment also protects anonymous speech.[9] When you stand on your digital soapbox, no one has to know who you are as long as you are otherwise acting within the confines of the law. For some, anonymity is a requirement for blogging about certain topics because of shame or potential repercussions. An example might be legal bloggers who write about the absurdities that occur in their law firms. The First Amendment generally respects and protects this need. It also protects your ability to use a pseudonym to leave comments on articles and blogs and while participating in chat rooms.

Two highly-read anonymous legal bloggers are known as BL1Y and The Namby Pamby. BL1Y writes for *Constitutional Daily*[10] and used to write for *BL1Y: The Life and Adventures of a Defunct Big Law Associate*.[11] The Namby Pamby writes for a blog named after his alter ego.[12] Both of these men have been selected for the American Bar Association's Top 100 Law Blawgs, but they can't add this honor to their resumes without revealing their true identities. They write about their experience as lawyers, including interactions with

---

8.   Reno v. ACLU, 521 U.S. 844, 870 (1997).

9.   Buckley v. Am. Constitutional Law Foundation, 525 U.S. 182, 200 (1999).

10.   *Constitutional Daily*, last visited August 6, 2013, http://www.constitutionaldaily.com/.

11.   *BL1Y: The Life and Adventures of a Defunct Big Law Associate*, last visited August 6, 2013, http://bl1y.com/.

12.   *The Namby Pamby*, last visited August 6, 2013, http://thenambypambyblog.com/.

the firm's partners, clients, and opposing counsels, which may put them at risk of losing their jobs or possibly being fired by their clients if their blogging identities became known.

If you want to be an anonymous blogger, you will have to maintain the division between your real life and your online persona. When you purchase your domain, you should use an e-mail address different from your work or personal e-mail addresses. The name of your blog should also not give away your identity. You should never post pictures of yourself that show your face or identifiable features or any content that might give your identity away.

When you are an anonymous blogger, your name and face may be concealed online; however, your IP address will always reveal what Internet source you used when you published a post, so your identity is traceable in many circumstances. To avoid this possibility, you might consider posting blog posts and doing all the work on your website while using public Wi-Fi in coffee shops, hotels, and libraries. You could also disguise your identity by creating an alter ego using a fake name generator.[13] You could disguise your location by using a proxy server, which masks where you are, geographically. Wael Ghonim successfully and frequently used a proxy server so that the Egyptian government could not identify or locate him while he was orchestrating protest activities through a Facebook page that led to the removal of then- president Hosni Mubarak in 2011.[14] The proxy server allowed him to work from Dubai while anyone who was monitoring him would perceive him as being in a different country.

---

13.   See Fake Name Generator™, last visited August 6, 2013, http://www.fakenamegenerator.com/.
14.   Wael Ghonim, *Revolution 2.0: The Power of the People is Greater than the People in Power: A Memoir*, Houghton Mifflin Harcourt, 2012.

NOT ALL SPEECH IS PROTECTED

The First Amendment protects free speech including controversial and inflammatory speech, but it does not protect all speech. Just like it doesn't give you the right to yell "fire" in a crowded theater, the First Amendment does not protect speech that is used to incite "imminent lawless action"[15] or speech that contains "fighting words,"[16] a "true threat"[17] or threats of violence.[18]

It would be unlikely that a lawyer would publish a blog post that would be viewed as a threat by a reader. If such a post is published, it would most likely be a situation where a lawyer is expressing his frustration with a situation, perhaps a co-worker or opposing counsel, and makes a statement that would lead the target to fear for his physical safety.

It's pretty hard to have "fighting words" in a blog post. These are "personally abusive epithets which, when addressed to the ordinary citizen, are, as a matter of common knowledge, inherently likely to provoke violent reaction."[19] They typically exist only in face-to-face interactions, and your fighting words must be about the person you're talking to.[20] It's best to think of fighting words as verbal attacks that will result in you being immediately punched in the face. The court will consider the content of the message and the context in which it was used. It's hard to make an argument that a blog contains fighting words because you might be angered by a blogger's words but, in most cases, you can't immediately hit him in response.

---

15.   Citizen Publishing Co. v. Miller, 115 P.3d 107, 112 (Ariz. 2005).
16.   Chaplinksy v. New Hampshire, 315 U.S. 568, 572 (1942).
17.   Virginia v. Black, 538 U.S. 343, 359 (2003).
18.   R.A.V. v. City of St. Paul, 505 U.S. 377, 388 (1992).
19.   Cohen v. California, 403 U.S. 15, 20 (1971).
20.   Chaplinksy at 573; Cohen at 20.

True threats are also not protected by the First Amendment. These are "statements where the speaker means to communicate a serious expression of intent to commit an act of unlawful violence to a particular individual or group of individuals."[21] Whether a statement is a true threat is determined by considering the statement in its context.[22] The speaker doesn't have to intend to carry out the threat, he only has to communicate a credible threat. These are incidents where the law cares more about what you said, not what you meant. If you wrote a post that you intended to be viewed as sarcastic, but readers interpreted as making a serious threat, you could face legal consequences because of it.

True threats, like fighting words, generally are not present in blog posts. Looking at pertinent court cases on this issue, a statement in a blog post, newspaper article, or letter to the editor is part of public discourse, and far less likely than a private communication or an in-person confrontation to be a true threat.[23]

Despite these limitations on speech, the majority of what you likely wish to say on your blog is protected by the First Amendment. It is often permissible to be blunt, even rude or cruel, in your writings. If you write for another person or organization's website, you might have editors that encourage you to write inflammatory posts. I have written my fair share of rants on all the blogs I regularly write for, and the feedback I usually hear is that the reader feels validated that I wrote about the thoughts and feelings he experienced. Sometimes in these posts, I swear. Unlike television and radio where there are words you must never use, no such list exists in the blogging world. If you want to say the *f*-word, the *s*-word, the *c*-word, or the *n*-word, it could hurt your reputation, but it's unlikely that using one of those words will be illegal.

---

21. Black at 359–60.
22. Citizen Publishing Co. at 114, citing Black at 345.
23. Citizen Publishing Co at 115, citing Melugin v. Hames, 38 F.3d 1478, 1484–85 (9th Cir. 1994); McCalden v. Cal. Library Ass'n, 955 F.2d 1214, 1222 (9th Cir. 1990).

Everyone in the United States is limited by the bounds of the First Amendment and other laws related to speech and investigative techniques. All publishers, whether commercial publishers or an individual with a blog, must follow all of these state and federal laws. Having a publication does not give you the "privilege to invade the rights and liberties of others."[24] If you are an anonymous blogger and you are sued because of your blog, your identity may be revealed through the discovery process. Once you are unmasked, you can't re-conceal yourself, and you may face other ramifications from people who are upset to learn that you are the person behind the posts.

All lawyers are bound by lawyer-client privilege. While you are allowed to share information that is in the public domain, you must be mindful when discussing your cases. You can talk about anything that is disclosed in open court, but you need to be careful that you don't inadvertently disclose something that was only revealed to you within the confines of a lawyer-client relationship. Likewise, you don't have to disclose to your clients that you're going to be sharing public information about them on your blog, but decorum dictates that it's good form to obtain their permission in advance and to speak about them only in general terms if they don't want to be mentioned by name on your website. Additionally, be careful if you want to use hidden cameras and/or other spy equipment to gather information for your blog, as that may be illegal in your state.

Furthermore, you want to be sure that you are not acting in ways that could lead to someone filing a bar complaint against you. If you write about a client, co-worker, opposing counsel, or judge, and he is offended by what you wrote, you will be at higher risk of facing discipline from your state bar.

---

24. Associated Press v. NLRB, 301 U.S. 103, 132–33 (1937).

THE DIFFERENCE BETWEEN FACT AND OPINION

When you're writing your posts, it's important for you to be aware of and distinguish between facts you are stating and opinions you are giving. You could face serious accusations and repercussions, such as a lawsuit for defamation, if you inadvertently state something as a fact when you meant to merely share an opinion. In these cases, your word selection matters more than what you intended to say.

When you create blog posts, your readers only have your words and perhaps the general nature of your blog to determine whether you are stating facts or opinions and whether you are being serious or sarcastic. They can't see your facial expression, hear the tone of your voice, or pick up on any other nonverbal cues that will reveal your motivation for creating a particular post.

It's not always easy to determine whether a statement contains facts or an opinion. If the opposing parties cannot agree whether a statement in question is a statement of fact or opinion, the court will make a determination for you. The court will consider the circumstances and context in which the statement was made.[25] Courts use a four-factor test to determine if a statement is a fact or an opinion:

1. the specific language used

2. whether the statement is verifiable

3. the general context of the statement within the publication

4. the broader context in which the statement appeared[26]

The court will examine the exact verbiage used in the statement, the nature of the blog post in which it was found, and the general nature of your entire blog. A court will be more likely to find that you have made a statement of fact if your work is generally non-fictional and serious than if your blog has a comedic or satirical purpose.

---

25. Scott v. News-Herald, 496 N.E.2d 699, 706 (1986).

26. Ollman v. Evans, 750 F.2d 970, 979 (1984), cert. denied 471 U.S. 1127 (1985).

The court may also rely on your state's laws regarding defamation and strategic lawsuits against public participation (SLAPP) to determine whether you stated a fact or an opinion. Anti-SLAPP laws are designed to combat frivolous lawsuits that have little chance of winning against defendants who exercise their First Amendment right to free speech.[27] These lawsuits are usually filed by plaintiffs with deep pockets who use the courts to intimidate journalists and bloggers into taking down critical articles and posts because they fear the costs of litigation.

Twenty-eight states have anti-SLAPP laws,[28] and the Electronic Frontier Foundation is advocating for Congress to pass a federal anti-SLAPP law that will protect the First Amendment rights of journalists, bloggers, and individuals who share their views as commenters or reviewers on others' websites. Without a federal anti-SLAPP law, there will always be a risk that bloggers will cave to the demands of plaintiffs who can afford to file baseless lawsuits to "censor and chill First Amendment protected speech."[29] A federal law would allow all bloggers to file a motion to dismiss if they ever face such a lawsuit.

---

27. Adi Kamdar, "The Case for a Federal Anti-SLAPP Statute," Electronic Frontier Foundation, Jul. 19, 2012, https://www.eff.org/deeplinks/2012/07/case-federal-anti-slapp-statute.

28. State Anti-SLAPP laws, Public Participation Project: Fighting for Free Speech, last visited August 6, 2013, http://www.anti-slapp.org/your-states-free-speech-protection/.

29. Trevor Timm, "New Federal Anti-SLAPP Legislation Introduced: A Good Start," Electronic Frontier Foundation, August 27, 2013, https://www.eff.org/deeplinks/2012/08/new-federal-anti-slapp-legislation-introduced-good-start.

IN SUMMARY

- The First Amendment protects the majority of what legal bloggers want to write on their blogs.

- You have the right to blog anonymously, but it comes with the responsibility of maintaining your anonymity.

- Be mindful and diligent to understand when you are stating a fact or stating an opinion.

Chapter 2
COPYRIGHT BASICS

When you write a blog post, your original thoughts are contained in your work. The law gives you rights to your work and provides options for recourse against other people who try to claim your work as their own or use it without your permission. The authority behind the copyright laws originates in the United States Constitution, which gives Congress the power to "promote the progress of science and useful arts, by securing for limited times to authors and inventors the exclusive right to their respective writings and discoveries."[30] Congress used this power to create the Copyright Act.

The Copyright Act protects authors' rights to the works they create.[31] This law applies to all "original works of authorship fixed in any tangible medium of expression, now known or later developed, from which they can be perceived, reproduced, or otherwise communicated, either directly or with the aid of a machine or device." A fixed tangible medium is any form that can be perceived for a period of time. Books, paintings, and photographs are fixed tangible mediums, but so is an ice sculpture. It may melt in a matter of hours, but

---

30. U.S. Constitution, Art. I, Sec. 8, cl. 8.
31. U.S. Copyright Act, 17 U.S.C. §§ 100 et seq. (2012).

for a period of time, it was fixed in a medium that you could perceive. Likewise, a computer file is a fixed tangible medium whether it's on a USB drive, a hard drive, or a server.

Copyrightable works include literary works, videos, infographics, and photographs. A blog post is usually a combination of words, images, and/or videos, which are all copyrightable works. Once your post is saved in any form, the Copyright Act protects it.

A work does not have to be registered with the United States Copyright Office to receive copyright protection. It is protected by the Copyright Act as soon as it is fixed in a tangible medium. Therefore, you have copyright rights to a blog post the second you create it as long as it's your original work.

COPYRIGHT RIGHTS

You obtain several exclusive rights when you fix your original work in a tangible medium. The Copyright Act gives you the exclusive right to reproduce your work; to publicly perform your work; to sell, rent, lease, or lend others copies of your work; and to create derivative works based on your original work. When it comes to your blog, the Copyright Act gives you the power to control where your content is seen, and it gives you the ability to exclude others from using your work without your permission. For example, if a bar association wanted to share one of your blog posts on its blog or in its newsletter, it would need to obtain your permission for a reprint. You may use any of your rights given to you by the Copyright Act. You can also give, sell, and/or license some or all of your rights to others.

The best way to think about copyright is to imagine a bundle of sticks where each stick represents one of your exclusive rights to your work. You may use as many of your sticks as you want. You may choose to use some sticks and not others. You may share, loan, give, or sell one or more of your sticks to other people.

Owning a work is not the same as owning the copyright to a work. If you buy a painting from an artist, legally, you have bought a "copy" of the artist's work, but the artist retains his copyright. Owning the painting gives you the right to display it in your home or to sell your painting to someone else, but it doesn't give you the right to make additional copies of it and sell them. In terms of blog posts, a reader who sees your website may read work and share the link to it with others. The reader is not permitted to copy your work onto their website or to print your work on paper and distribute it widely without your consent.

WHAT IS A DERIVATIVE WORK?

A derivative work is a work that is based on one or more preexisting works such as a "translation, musical arrangement, dramatization, fictionalization, motion picture version, sound recording, art reproduction, abridgment, condensation, or any other form in which a work may be recast, transformed, or adapted."[32] For example, J.K. Rowling obtained the copyright to the Harry Potter books when she wrote them. The Harry Potter movies are derivative works of J.K. Rowling's books. Warner Brothers could not create them without her permission. Likewise, George Lucas owned the copyrights for the Star Wars movies. Derivative works of these films include the Star Wars action figures, Yoda backpacks, posters, costumes, and light saber toys. When Lucas sold Lucasfilm to the Walt Disney Company in 2012, Disney acquired the rights to the Star Wars franchise and now controls what derivative works can be made based on the films.

A blog could have derivative works. It could be a sibling blog to your original blog or a book that compiles previously published blog posts. Likewise, if you post drawings or photographs on your blog,

---

32.   17 U.S.C. § 101 (2012).

and you create a line of products based on your work, those would be derivative works. Matt Inman, better known as The Oatmeal, sells books, posters, mugs, t-shirts, magnets, stickers, and prints that are based on the comics he released on his website.[33] These are all derivative works.

AUTOMATIC COPYRIGHT PROTECTION

You have a copyright to your work the second it's fixed in a tangible medium. You do not have to put the ©, "copyright [year]," or register your work with the Copyright Office to get legal protection for your work. The law protects you the moment a work is created. You, as the copyright owner, have the right to sell or give the copyright to your work to someone else. Traditional book authors are often required to do this. They relinquish their copyright to their publishers in exchange for getting their work published and receiving royalty payments.

J.K. Rowling had the copyright to her books when she wrote them. She probably signed over some of these rights to Bloomsbury Publishing and Scholastic to get them published. When Warner Brothers wanted to make the books into movies, they had to get permission from the publishers to make the derivative works, because the publishers owned the copyright. Likewise, J.K. Rowling retained the digital rights for her Harry Potter novels; she is using those rights to release e-books through *Pottermore*.[34]

---

33.   The Oatmeal, last visited August 6, 2013, http://shop.theoatmeal.com/.
34.   *Pottermore*, last visited August 6, 2013, http://www.pottermore.com/.

COPYRIGHT APPLIES TO EXPRESSION, NOT IDEAS OR FACTS

When you have a copyright, that protection applies only to your exact expression, not to any of the ideas underlying or contained in your work. Another person cannot copy your exact verbiage and claim it as his own; however, other writers are permitted to write about the same ideas that you write about. For example, if you have a personal injury law blog, you might write a blog post about the benefits of having uninsured and underinsured motorist insurance. Writing this post does not give you the right to prevent other people from writing about the benefits of having uninsured and underinsured motorist insurance, even if the writer uses the same real-life example to demonstrate his points. If the other blogger copies one of your posts, republishes it, and claims to be the author, that's copyright infringement and you have options for recourse.

In addition, facts are not protected under the Copyright Act.[35] Originally, the Copyright Act protected people who put energy and effort into creating works even if they had no original expression. Under this old rule, phone books (i.e., alphabetized lists of names, addresses, and phone numbers) were copyrightable. This rule changed in 1991 with *Feist Publications, Inc. v. Rural Telephone Service Co.*[36]

Rural Telephone Service was a public telephone company, and it was required to publish a phone book for its subscribers. Feist Publications was an independent company that published phone books that covered broader areas. It wanted to combine eleven phone books into one big phone book. Feist sought licenses from each phone service provider for their listings. Rural refused to let Feist copy its listings and, unfortunately for Feist, Rural's service area was in the middle of the geographic area Feist wanted to include in its

---

35. Feist Publications, Inc. v. Rural Telephone Service Co., 499 U.S. 340, 344 (1991).
36. *Id.*

phone book. Despite not having Rural's permission, Feist copied Rural's listings into its phone book. Rural sued for copyright infringement and argued that Feist wrongfully stole its information. The court ruled that phone books were a list of facts in an unoriginal arrangement and that facts alone were not copyrightable.

The Copyright Act can protect an arrangement of facts if the arrangement is original. There's no copyright protection in an arrangement of facts that's unoriginal or does not contain any original expression. In the *Feist* case, there was no originality in an alphabetical arrangement of names and phone numbers; thus, it did not qualify for copyright protection.

The court has also ruled that copying facts from another writer's website does not constitute copyright infringement. In the case of *Silver v. Lavandeira*, Elizabeth Silver sued Mario Lavandeira, better known as Perez Hilton, and accused him of stealing copyrighted information from her website and posting it on his blog.[37] She filed a motion for an injunction that would have forced Hilton to remove the material he copied from her site. Silver had the burden of proving that Hilton copied her original content to win the case. The court ruled that Hilton copied only facts from Silver's website. Since Hilton did not copy any of Silver's original expression, there was no copyright infringement.

To look back at the personal injury blog example, if you wrote a post about benefits of uninsured and underinsured motorist insurance, the expression of your opinion and experiences with this topic would be protected under the Copyright Act. However, a quote from your state's minimum insurance requirements is simply a statement of facts, and therefore that information could not be protected by copyright. You could register your copyright to that blog post but you couldn't sue someone for copyright infringement if he copied only the facts from your post.

---

37. Silver v. Lavandeira, 2009 WL 513031, *1 (S.D.N.Y. 2009).

TRANSFERRING A COPYRIGHT

When you create a work, you automatically get the exclusive copyright to your work. The copyright include the ability to give, lease, and/or sell some or all of your rights to someone else. Copyrights can be transferred just like any other property you own. This is usually accomplished with a contract.

The transfer of a copyright can be exclusive or nonexclusive. If you transfer one or all of your rights exclusively to one person or entity, the transfer must be in writing and signed by you (or your agent). When you exclusively transfer your copyright to another person, you can no longer use those rights. The person you transferred them to is the only person who has the right to use your work based on the right(s) you transferred to him.

A nonexclusive transfer of a copyright occurs when you give someone permission to use one of your rights, but you still retain the same right yourself. You can give nonexclusive right transfers for one of your rights to multiple persons if you wish. Nonexclusive transfers of copyright do not have to be in writing.

An example of a nonexclusive transfer of a right is if someone liked one of your blog posts and asked to republish the content on his website or newsletter. If you give him a nonexclusive license to use your right to copy your work, you would give him permission to copy your content but you would retain the right to allow others to republish your work on other sites and you could republish it yourself in other publications.

Transferring rights is similar to giving or selling any other type of personal property. Your state's laws regarding property transfers, inheritance, contracts, and businesses may affect your ability to transfer your copyrights. Please consult the applicable statutes and case law in your state to ensure that your transfer complies with your state's laws.

When you make an exclusive transfer of some or all of the copyright to your work, you can record the contract with the Copyright Office. The Copyright Office keeps the records of transfers it receives and makes them available for public inspection; however, it does not enforce these agreements and it cannot determine whether the contract is valid. If there is an issue regarding the transfer, that is an issue between you and the other party. The Copyright Office is simply an optional depository for the record. If there is a dispute regarding who owns a particular right to a work, having a copy of the contract that transferred the right(s) on file at the Copyright Office can be used as prima facie evidence that the transfer occurred.

If you decide after you have transferred your copyright to another person or entity that you want it back, in many cases you will have to purchase the copyright back from them. There are situations where it is more lucrative to purchase your rights back to use them for other opportunities or to sell them to someone else who can make you a better offer—such as if a publisher wanted to publish a collection of your blog posts, including content with rights that you had previously transferred to someone else. Be wary that there is always the possibility that the person you transferred your rights to will decline your offer to purchase your rights back, and there is usually nothing you can do in such a situation.

Your copyright for any works created after January 1, 1978, will exist for seventy years after your death. (When a company creates a copyrightable work, the copyright rights last for one hundred twenty years from the date of creation.) This means that your copyrights will be part of your estate, and you must decide who will own them after you die. If you do not specifically state who owns your copyrights in your will, they will pass to your family according to your state's intestacy laws, which apply when a person dies without a will, or via the residuary clause in your will if it has such a clause. Your residuary clause is a provision of your will that states who will own the parts of your estate that you don't account for in your will. If you want copyrights for your works to go to specific individuals when you die, work with an estate planner to draft the proper documents to accomplish this.

RELEASING YOUR WORK INTO THE PUBLIC DOMAIN

If your work was created after January 1, 1978, your copyright will last for seventy years after your death. At that time, your works will enter the public domain. When a work enters the public domain, no one owns the copyright to it, and anyone can use the work in any way. You may, of course, relinquish your works to the public domain at any time during your lifetime.

Releasing your work into the public domain is easy to do. You, as the copyright holder, must add a written statement to a work that states you release all your rights to the work. You can release all of your work to the public domain, or just specific works. Releasing your work into the public domain is permanent and irrevocable. You can never reclaim the copyright to your work again. Once you release it, the public owns it.

Some copyright holders wish to have their works released into the public domain when they die. If you want to do this, your best course of action is to release your work into the public domain yourself, prior to your death. If you release your works in your will, your family could contest your will and make arguments that you weren't of sound mind when you wrote that provision and thus the court should disregard it. If the court accepts your family's argument, your works will be passed on according to the intestacy laws of your state or the residuary clause in your will. At that point, you'll be dead and you won't be able to advocate for yourself.

The best way to avoid all this drama, heartache, and legal expense among your surviving family members is to release your work into the public domain before you die. Your family can only fight over the property you own when you die. If you don't own your copyrights any more, they can't fight over them. Your family and friends can't claim a right to them because at that point the general public will own your works.

IN SUMMARY

- You obtain the copyright to your work the moment you have an original work of authorship that is fixed in any tangible medium.

- The Copyright Act gives the author the exclusive rights to copy, distribute, display, perform, and make derivative works based on your work.

- Your rights only apply to your exact expression, not to the ideas or facts contained in your work.

- For works created after January 1, 1978, a copyright held by an individual lasts for the life of the author plus seventy years. If the original owner is an entity, it lasts for one hundred twenty years from the date of creation.

Chapter 3

INTEGRATING OTHERS' WORK INTO YOUR BLOG

People rarely blog in a vacuum. You write about things that inspire, intrigue, and provoke you personally and professionally. As a lawyer, your blog is an excellent place to react and respond to current events related to your practice areas. To that end, you may want to quote others' blogs, news articles, books, and movies. It's common to want to use other people's content in your blog posts, but there is a right and a wrong way to do it under the Copyright Act.

FAIR USE

When people talk about using other people's content, the first thing they usually claim is "fair use." The fair use doctrine gives you the ability to incorporate other people's work in your work, but it's a little complicated. Fair use does not give you permission to use another person's work, but rather it gives you a defense that you can use if you're accused of infringing on someone else's copyright.

The fair use doctrine is an affirmative defense. When you claim that your copying of another's work is fair use, you're essentially saying, "Yes, I copied your work, but it's OK." When you rely on fair use to protect you, you always run the risk that the original author will claim that your use of his work infringes on his copyright and file a lawsuit. If that happens, you will have the burden of proving to the court that your use of the original author's work was protected.

Fair use gives you the ability to copy someone else's work if you build upon it with your own original thoughts or if you're using it to inform or educate. Generally, you are allowed to copy someone's work if you're criticizing or commenting on the original work, writing the news, teaching, or participating in scholarship or research. Fair use is the reason book and movie reviewers can include quotes or images from the work they're reviewing in their articles. It's also why teachers can make multiple photocopies of otherwise copyrighted works for use in the classroom.

In regard to blogging, you can often copy a portion of someone else's work into your blog under fair use if you add your own thoughts about the subject. It's also good etiquette to include an attribution to the original author and a link to the original source, so your readers can see the copied portion in its original context. If you copy the exact verbiage of another's work into your blog without adding any original thoughts of your own, that is likely copyright infringement and not protected by the Copyright Act because the copyright holder has the exclusive right to control where his work is reproduced. This is true even if you give an attribution to the original author.

If you are sued for copyright infringement and you want to claim that your use was protected by fair use, the court will consider four factors:

1. The purpose and character of the use
2. The nature of the copyrighted work that was copied
3. The amount and substantiality of the portion from the original work used compared to the whole copyrighted work

4. The effect of the use upon the potential market for or the value of the copyrighted work[38]

The court may consider other factors if the facts of the case merit it. If you have added your own original expression to the original work, such as your opinion about the author's work, the court may find that there is no copyright infringement and that your use is protected by fair use.

The court weighs all four factors in deciding whether your use qualifies as fair use; however, it mainly considers the effect on the potential market. The court is more likely to find that your use of another's work constitutes copyright infringement when consumers view your work as a viable substitute for the original you copied. There is no way to know for certain if your use is protected by fair use until the case is evaluated by a court unless you have permission from the copyright holder to publish the work.

One of the landmark fair use cases involved the controversial band, 2 Live Crew. In the early 1990s, 2 Live Crew wanted to release a parody of "Oh, Pretty Woman" by Roy Orbison and William Dees. The band offered to give the original authors an attribution and pay a fee to use the song, but Acuff-Rose Music, Inc., which owned the copyright, refused. 2 Live Crew used the song anyway, and Acuff-Rose sued for copyright infringement.[39]

The case was decided by the United States Supreme Court and 2 Live Crew won when the Court ruled that parodies were protected by fair use. A parody is unique in that it must imitate the original work to have the desired effect. You must walk a fine line between imitating enough to have the artistic effect you want but not copy the original so much that it constitutes infringement. In 2 Live Crew's case, they added their original expression to the existing

---

38.   17 U.S.C. § 107 (2012).
39.   Campbell, et al. v. Acuff-Rose Music, Inc., 510 U.S. 569, 571-72 (1994).

work and the market for their song was not the same market as the Roy Orbison version. No one would seek out a copy of the original song and accept 2 Live Crew's version as a substitute.

The purpose of the fair use doctrine is to promote the creation of original works that transform others' previous works. Copying an article, in part or in whole, on your blog, may be transformative enough to constitute fair use if you add enough of your own original thoughts to the copied portion. If you are going to do something like this, be aware of the possibility that your use may not constitute fair use but may be an illegal derivative work. If the portion you copied is a substitute for the original article itself, it's probably not fair use.

When you're selecting others' work to use in your blog, be aware of entities that purchase copyrights from others and file copyright infringement claims against anyone who copies any part of the work they own. These entities are sometimes referred to as "copyright trolls" because they appear to exist solely to acquire copyrights that others are likely to copy content from, and then to bring copyright infringement cases against anyone who uses any of this content in any way. One such entity to do this in recent years was Righthaven. Righthaven purchased the copyrights to the *Las Vegas Review Journal*. Righthaven sued blogger Michael Nelson when he copied a portion of an article from the *Las Vegas Review Journal* on his blog.[40]

Nelson responded to the lawsuit by arguing that his use of the article was protected by fair use. The court evaluated the case using the four fair use factors. The first fair use factor, the purpose and character of Nelson's blog, favored Righthaven. The purpose of Nelson's blog was to create business for himself, which is a commercial purpose. The other fair use factors favored Nelson's position. Nelson copied only eight sentences of a thirty-sentence article and the portion that he copied contained only facts about a new federal housing

---

40.   Righthaven, LLC v. Realty One Group, Inc., 2010 WL 4115413, *1 (D.Nev. 2010).

program. The court also found that Nelson's use of the copyrighted material would not have much effect on the market for the news article because none of the original author's commentary was copied. Therefore, Nelson's use of the article had little or no impact on Righthaven's ability to make money off the article and was not a substitute for Righthaven's article. The court held that Nelson's use of Righthaven's work was fair use and dismissed the case.

I've shared the Righthaven case with you for three reasons:

1. To warn you about copyright trolls and what they do
2. To show you that you can win a case against a copyright troll
3. To demonstrate the challenge and hassle that can accompany defending yourself against copyright infringement claims with a fair use argument

I don't want to discourage you from building on others' work, but I do want to encourage you to be thoughtful about whose work you copy. If you hear that a copyright troll has bought the rights to someone's content, you probably should stay away from it. Find other sources to quote. If you rely on the fair use doctrine to protect your ability to copy others' work, you may have to go to trial to win your case. Because the court has to evaluate your use using the four fair use factors, it is less likely that the case will be settled before trial.

Another word of caution: if you have ads on your blog, even if you don't earn much money from them, your use of another's work could be characterized as commercial. In the event that you are accused of copyright infringement and you argue that your use is fair use, the fact that you make money off your website could be a strike against you in the eyes of the court. The original author could argue that you copied his work in order to get more hits on your blog, and thus make more money from your ads. The more money you make off that particular blog post, the more likely the court will think that you copied another's work solely for your own financial gain.

Additionally, if your blog is part of your law firm's website, your blog exists for the commercial purpose of creating business for the firm. You need to be extra careful when using and building upon others' material.

CREATIVE COMMONS IMAGES

Visual images can enhance the message conveyed in your blog posts. One of the best sources for images is Creative Commons.[41] Creative Commons provides licenses for images and other content where the artist retains the copyright to his work but grants everyone certain permissions to use his work. Most licenses require you to give an attribution to the original artist if you use his work. Some licenses prohibit you from using the artist's work for commercial purposes, and others prohibit you from modifying the original work. The license may also come with a share-alike provision. If you use the work, you must offer it, with the same license provisions, to other people who wish to copy it. If you use an image in a way that does not comply with the requirements of the license, you will likely be committing copyright infringement.

Thousands of images are available with Creative Commons licenses, so there is no reason for you to have boring images on your blog, or a blog post without an image.

When you select images for your blog from Creative Commons, always pick images that have a license that allows you to modify and commercialize them. This license gives you the most freedom. You want to have the ability to modify images so you can crop them to fit your needs. If your blog is part of a law firm's website, it has a commercial purpose; therefore, you need images that you can commercialize. If you own a legal blog that is separate from a law firm's website, you may not be making any money from it now, but you

---

41.   Creative Commons, last visited August 6, 2013, www.CreativeCommons.org.

might in the future. You don't want to have to take the time to review every image on your website to determine which images you have to replace so you can commercialize your work.

If you cannot find the image you want under Creative Commons, you can purchase the right to use other photos through companies like iStock, Shutter Stock, and Getty Images.

WHEN IN DOUBT, ASK PERMISSION

If there is an image or any content that you want to use that doesn't come with a license for you to use it on your blog, you can always ask the copyright holder for permission to use his work. I know incredible photographers who usually post their work on Flickr with all their copyrights reserved. They have never said "no" when I've asked them if I could use a photo on my blog. They simply require that I give them an attribution and a link to the original photo, which I'm always happy to do. Three photographers have given me permission to use any of their work in this way, regardless of what license they attach to their work on Flickr.

When I was in law school, I was frequently unhappy with the school's administration and I would write about my dissatisfaction on my blog. I wanted to include a picture of the dean of the law school at that time. I didn't have a picture of him, and I knew I'd be committing copyright infringement and face at least a cease-and-desist letter if I used a picture from the school's website. I did a search on Flickr and found one image of the dean of my school, but it was posted with all rights reserved. I sent a message to the copyright holder and told him that I was writing a blog about the dean and asked if I could use his image. The owner responded that I could use it and told me what attribution he wanted to appear with it. The copyright owner never asked about the details of the post, and never said anything to me that indicates that he saw or was unhappy about the post where the image appeared.

IN SUMMARY

- The fair use provision of the Copyright Act allows you to use others' work so long as you are using it in a transformative way or adding your original thoughts to it. Providing an attribution without adding any original content is not sufficient.

- Fair use is a defense, not a permission slip.

- When in doubt, get permission from the author to use his work, or use content that comes with a Creative Commons license.

Chapter 4
COPYRIGHT REGISTRATION

Although you automatically get copyright protection the instant your original expression is fixed in a tangible medium (i.e., you save your blog on your computer), there are benefits for some bloggers in registering their blog with the United States Copyright Office. You can register each post individually or you can try to register all your posts as a single work. Every work that is registered with the Copyright Office is placed in the Library of Congress, the world's largest library.

The Copyright Act protects a work only *after* it is created and fixed in a tangible medium. The law cannot give you copyright protection for works that do not exist; therefore, the Copyright Act can protect works on the Internet, including blogs, only after they are created. You cannot register your blog once and have every subsequent post you add to it be protected by the Copyright Act under that single registration.

HOW TO REGISTER YOUR BLOG

The Copyright Act was written before blogs existed; and thus, it can be difficult to determine which category you should use when registering your blog with the Copyright Office.[42] Each individual blog post can be treated as a separate work that can be registered with the Copyright Office. You will have to select the proper registration form based on what type of expression is in your post. If your blog post contains mainly words, it's a literary work. If it's mainly photographs or drawings, it's a pictorial work. If your blog is mainly photographs, you should talk with your lawyer about whether you should register each blog post as a work or each image as a separate work. If your blog is mainly videos, it's a motion picture. If you are confused about how to categorize you work, you should call the Copyright Office or review the circulars on the Copyright Office's website.

A copyright for a single work can be registered via the Copyright Office website by submitting an application and fee.[43] As of this writing (October 2013) the cost to register a single work electronically is $35. With your application, you must include a copy of your work, which will be deposited in the Library of Congress. For blogs that are literary works, you may submit your work in hard copy by printing out a copy of the blog post you want to register, or you can submit it electronically.

Registering every blog post you create individually can be time consuming and expensive. If you treat each post as a separate work, you will have to submit each post separately with a separate application and $35 fee. If you publish a new blog post every week, it will cost at least $1820 to register all of your individual posts for a year.

---

42. U.S. Copyright Office, Information Circulars and Factsheets, last visited August 6, 2013, http://www.copyright.gov/circs/.

43. U.S. Copyright Office Fee Schedule, last visited August 6, 2013, http://www.copyright.gov/docs/fees.html.

BLOGS ARE NOT SERIAL WORKS

If you post new blogs at regular intervals, and you read the Copyright Act, you might think that your blog qualifies as a serial work.[44] Serial works include "periodicals, newspapers, magazines, bulletins, newsletters, annuals, journals, proceedings of societies, and other similar works." Serial works have to be registered every three months using a single application and a $65 fee. If you published a blog post every week and registered it as a serial work, it would cost only $260 for a year's worth of posts.

Unfortunately, through a representative, the Copyright Office claims that blogs do not qualify as serial works. The office claims that "group registration is not available for electronic journals published one article at a time because such works are not collective works."[45] Even if a blog were allowed to be registered as a serial work, you could register only those works that are published according to your publication schedule. If you published a special blog post on a day you didn't usually publish, you would likely have to register its copyright separately from the serial registration.

With so many publications foregoing paper printing in lieu of being strictly online publications, this rule may change. A blogger who writes a weekly or monthly blog on a strict schedule may have a valid claim that blogs should be treated like other online magazines or newsletters. If these works that are serial works when published on paper are allowed to continue to be registered as serial works if they are only released digitally, then blogs that focus on a particular topic or set of themes and publish according to a schedule should be treated as serial works under the law.

---

44. U.S. Copyright Office, Circular 62B, Copyright Registration for a Group of Serial Issues, last visited August 6, 2013, http://www.copyright.gov/circs/circ62b.pdf.
45. United States Copyright Office, Circular 66: Copyright Registration for Online Works, last visited August 6, 2013, http://www.copyright.gov/circs/circ66.pdf.

BLOGS MIGHT BE DERIVATIVE WORKS

In a previous conversation, a representative for the Copyright Office stated that the entire content of a blog could be registered as a single work and every subsequent registration could be filed to register any new content that was added to the website. Each subsequent registration would be a derivative work of the original work. The representative said that each registration should include the previous registered material; however, the Copyright Office website states that the new registrations should exclude any previously registered material.[46]

Registering your blog as a derivative work appears to be a cost effective way to protect your copyright. You can register your blog as a literary work for $35 if you submit your application electronically. If you registered the new content added to your blog as a derivative work every three months, it would only cost $140 to register a year's worth of posts, which is much cheaper than registering each post individually.

I can say from experience that the Copyright Office will let you register multiple blog posts as a single work, but recent conversations with the Copyright Office showed that they frown upon this practice. You will see below why this might not be the best course of action if you expect to sue for copyright infringement and collect statutory damages if your work is stolen. A representative stated that you may not register the same post as a single work and as part of a larger work.

WHEN IS A BLOG PUBLISHED?

The Copyright Act states that you must register your work within three months of publication or within one month of learning that

---

46. *Id.*

your copyright has been infringed (whichever happens first) to be able to collect statutory damages and lawyers' fees.[47] It's because of this rule that you might think it's in your best interest to register your blog every three months. When a work is unpublished, it must be registered with the Copyright Office prior to the infringement for the copyright holder to be eligible for statutory damages and lawyers' fees.

Thinking logically, you might think that a blog post is published once it is released on your website where anyone on the Internet can see it. However, the Copyright Office defines publication as "the distribution of copies or phonorecords of a work to the public by sale or other transfer ownership, or by rental, lease, or lending."[48] Offering to distribute copies "for the purpose of further distribution, public performance, or public display" also constitutes publication.[49] Based on this definition, works that are only available on the Internet are likely not published under the Copyright Act. Therefore, blogs are unpublished works, regardless of your readership. You have to register your work with the Copyright Office only if you want to sue suspected infringers for copyright infringement and to collect statutory damages and lawyers' fees. If you do not want to sue alleged infringers for copyright infringement or if you want to collect only your actual damages, you do not need to register your work with Copyright Office in advance.

SHOULD YOU REGISTER YOUR BLOG COPYRIGHTS?

Although the Copyright Act gives you copyright protection for your work as soon as you create it, certain remedies are available only if

---

47.   17 U.S.C. § 408 (2012).

48.   United States Copyright Office, Circular 1: Copyright Basics, last visited August 6, 2013, http://www.copyright.gov/circs/circ01.pdf.

49.   *Id.*

your work is registered with the Copyright Office.[50] In particular, you cannot file a lawsuit for copyright infringement unless your work has been registered. Since most blog content does not qualify as a "publication," your work must be registered prior to the infringement occurring to be eligible for statutory damages.[51] Statutory damages may be as little as $200, but may be as much as $150,000 per violation if there is willful infringement. Willful infringement means the infringer knew that he was illegally copying your copyrighted material.

You can always sue for your actual damages if you register your work with the Copyright Office after your work has been infringed. This is the amount of money that you didn't earn because of the infringement or the amount of money that your infringer made by copying your work.

Many people in these situations have no actual damages because they don't make any money from their blogs. If you make money from ads on your blog, you can collect the amount of income that you didn't make from your ads due to the infringement, which could be a miniscule amount. Likewise, if the person who infringed your work is making money from the infringement, the actual damages would include the amount of money that he earned because of your content. Unless a successful blogger stole your work, this amount is likely to be low as well.

If your copyright is registered prior to the infringement, you may also be eligible for lawyers' fees. This means that if you win, the other party has to pay the fees you owe to your lawyer. Without lawyers' fees, it may not be worth it to sue for copyright infringement because you may owe your lawyer more money than the amount you were awarded by the court if you win the case.

---

50.   17 U.S.C. §§ 411-12 (2012).

51.   17 U.S.C. § 412 (2012).

If you registered multiple blog posts as one work and one of your posts was infringed after registration, you could sue for copyright infringement. The challenge with this scenario is you will likely be awarded a lower amount of damages than if you had registered each post individually. For example, if you registered one hundred blog posts as one literary work and only one of those posts was subsequently posted on someone else's website without your consent, you could sue for copyright infringement and request statutory damages. However, you would be arguing that you deserve compensation because someone stole one percent of your work. It would be much easier for the alleged infringer to defend himself by arguing that he only used a de minimus amount of what you claimed to be one literary work. Conversely, had you registered each post separately and one post was replicated on another website, you could sue for copyright infringement and be more likely to be awarded a larger amount of statutory damages because one hundred percent of what you claimed to be one literary work was copied without your consent.

Based on this information, you may wonder if it is worthwhile to register your blog content with the Copyright Office. In many situations it is not cost effective. However, if you have posts that you expect will be illegally copied, especially if they are likely to be copied by someone who has the ability to pay thousands of dollars in statutory damages and your lawyers' fees, it may be prudent to register each of those posts as individual works. If you wish to register a post with the Copyright Office, you should do it prior to releasing the post on your website to ensure that your work was registered prior to the infringement. You only need to submit your application to the Copyright Office prior to releasing it online; you do not need your certificate of registration from the Copyright Office to guarantee that you have preserved the option to sue for copyright infringement and to request statutory damages and lawyers' fees.

Additionally, you only need to register your work with the Copyright Office if you want to sue for copyright infringement. Many bloggers who discover that others are illegally reproducing their work are not interested in pursuing a lawsuit. They either want their material removed from the infringing website or they want proper credit for their work. If you will allow others to reproduce your work as long as the person gives you an attribution, you should consider adding a Creative Commons license to your work, or terms of service to your website that provide instructions on how others can use your work.

REGISTERING A BLOG WRITTEN ANONYMOUSLY OR PSEUDONYMOUSLY

Some legal bloggers write anonymously or use a pseudonym. These bloggers include The Namby Pamby[52] and BL1Y.[53] This practice is perfectly acceptable because your First Amendment right to free speech extends to anonymous speech. There will always be ways to trace your blog back to you via the Internet service you used or your domain registration; however, you do not have to disclose your true identity to copyright a blog post. If you register your work, you must check the "Pseudonymous" box when you provide information about the work's author(s). The Copyright Office requires you to provide information about your citizenship or domicile, which will reveal some evidence regarding your true identity.

If you wish, you may list your legal name and your pseudonym on your copyright registration. The names of the work's authors become part of the Copyright Office's public records, so do not give your legal name if you want to keep your identity a secret. Once your name is added to the public record, it cannot be removed.

---

52.   *The Namby Pamby, supra* note 12.

53.   BL1Y, *The Constitutional Daily,* last visited August 6, 2013, http://www.constitutionaldaily.com/index.php?option=com_content&view=article&id=68:bl1y&catid=41:authors&Itemid=66

When you register a work using a pseudonym, your copyright protection lasts ninety-five years from publication of the work or one hundred twenty years from the work's creation, whichever comes first. If your identity is revealed in the Copyright Office's registration records, including other copyright registrations, your copyright term becomes the length of your life, plus seventy years.

IN SUMMARY

- It is confusing to determine the best way to register a blog with the Copyright Office. Each post must be registered individually because blogs do not qualify as serial works.

- Most blogs do not qualify as "published"; therefore, you must register a post before infringement occurs to be eligible for statutory damages.

- For most bloggers, it is not worth it to register your blogs' copyrights with the Copyright Office because infringement is unlikely to occur, and if it does, the actual damages will be minimal and/or the infringer will likely be unable to pay statutory damages.

Chapter 5
PROTECTING YOUR COPYRIGHT

Once you have a copyright, no one is allowed to copy, distribute, display, perform, or make derivative works based on your work without your permission. When you write blog posts, you have an obligation to make sure that you're not copying others' work on your blog, including inadvertent copying. Likewise, other writers and artists have the responsibility to not purposely or inadvertently copy your work.

It's possible for someone to copy someone else's work without realizing it, and be held liable for copyright infringement. For example, when George Harrison wrote "My Sweet Lord," he claimed he did not intend to plagiarize "He's So Fine" by The Chiffons. However, when the court compared the two songs, it found that the music was almost identical. The court suggested that Harrison copied the song because he retained it in his subconscious.[54] They ruled that Harrison committed copyright infringement and ordered him to pay a licensing fee for copying The Chiffons' music.

---

54. Bright Tunes Music Corp. v. Harrisongs Music, LTD, 420 F.Supp. 177, 180 (D.C.N.Y. 1976).

POLICING THE INTERNET FOR COPYRIGHT INFRINGEMENT

The best way to ensure that no one is copying content from your blog without your permission is to police the Internet for unauthorized copying of your work. You can do this for free using Google Alerts. You can set up alerts for key phrases and sentences from posts that you suspect will be copied by other writers. Some writers purposely put spelling or grammar mistakes in their work that will make it easier for them to detect copying because the infringer will incorporate the mistake into the infringing work. A punctuation mistake that may go unnoticed is a double period at the end of a sentence.. In the *Feist* case, Rural Telephone Service was able to prove that Feist copied its phone book because Rural had four fake entries in its listing. When Feist copied Rural's directory into its phone book, it incorporated Rural's fake entries.

If you post original images on your blog, you can use the Google Images search engine to search for your images.[55] You can search for your images using the image's URL or by uploading the file to the search engine.[56]

There are also websites that can assist you in detecting plagiarism online, such as Copyscape,[57] DOC Cop,[58] and Reprint Writers.[59] Some of these services require registration and payment to search for larger blocks of text. They all have free versions available but the search parameters may be limited, and you may only be able to use the search tool a limited number of times each day.

---

55.   Google Images, last visited May 30, 2013, http://www.google.com/imghp.
56.   Ruth Carter, "Using Google Image Search to Detect Copyright Infringement," Carter Law Firm, Mar. 21, 2013, http://carterlawaz.com/2013/03/using-google-image-search-to-detect-copyright-infringement/.
57.   Copyscape, last visited May 30, 2013, http://www.copyscape.com/.
58.   DOC Cop, last visited May 30, 2013, http://www.doccop.com.
59.   Reprint Writers, last visited May 30, 2013, http://www.reprintwriters.com/copyright-checker/check.php.

Another strategy for detecting copyright infringement of your content is to monitor your website's analytics, which provides information about how readers get to your website. Some people will plagiarize your work and think that it is permissible as long as they provide a link and possibly an attribution to the original site. When a reader views the website where your work is being plagiarized and follows the link to view the original content on your website, the information about the allegedly infringing site will be in your analytics. You should check your analytics regularly and research any unfamiliar websites that are leading people to your website to check for infringement.

DIGITAL MILLENNIUM COPYRIGHT ACT

The Digital Millennium Copyright Act (DMCA) is a provision in the Copyright Act that is designed to create a "safe harbor" for websites like YouTube, which allow users to post their own content to the site. According to YouTube, seventy-two hours of video are uploaded to YouTube every minute.[60] There's no way that Google, which owns YouTube, can verify that each video is not violating someone's copyright. The DMCA affords companies like Google a way to protect themselves from copyright infringement lawsuits. The DMCA also applies to companies that host websites, such as DreamHost.

To qualify for DMCA protection, a website that hosts content must register a DMCA agent with the Copyright Office. A DMCA agent is the designated person who receives DMCA takedown notices from people who suspect their work is being infringed on that website. The purpose of a DMCA takedown notice is to inform the company hosting the site that your copyright is allegedly being infringed on one of their sites and to direct the company to remove

---

60.   YouTube, Statistics, last visited May 27, 2013, http://www.youtube.com/yt/press/statistics.html.

or disable access to the suspected infringing material. When the agent receives a DMCA takedown notice, he must act expeditiously to remove the public's access to the material.[61]

Sending a DMCA takedown notice is often the most efficient way to remove your content that has been posted without your consent on another's website. You do not have to confront the person who you suspect copied your content and published it on his site. Instead, you bypass him and work directly with the company that hosts his site.

If you suspect that someone is infringing your copyright and you want to send a DMCA takedown notice, start by looking up which company hosts the website where you found the infringement. This is easily accomplished using WhoIs.com, a database that provides information regarding who registered website domains ending in *.com*, *.org*, and *.net*. Your search results will tell you which company the infringer used when he created his website. You should verify this information using IP-Lookup.net, which will provide information regarding the company that is hosting the website. In some instances, the website owner registered the domain with one company and is using another company to host the website.

Next, go to the Copyright Office website and look up the hosting company's registered DMCA agent.[62] The listing will tell you the company's DMCA agent's name and the address or e-mail address where you have to send your DMCA takedown notice. If you do not send the takedown notice to the company's DMCA agent, the company does not have to comply with it.

Then, you need to send a DMCA takedown notice to the company's registered agent. The law requires that for the takedown notice

---

61.   17 U.S.C. § 512(c)(1) (2012).
62.   U.S. Copyright Office, Directory of Service Provider Agents for Notification of Claims of Infringement, last visited July 25, 2013, http://www.copyright.gov/onlinesp/.

to be valid, it must be in writing and include all of the following information:

1. Your physical or electronic signature

2. The identity of your work that is allegedly being infringed

3. The specific URL for the website where the infringement is occurring

4. Your contact information (i.e., your address, telephone number, and/or e-mail address)

5. A "statement that the complaining party has a good faith belief that use of the material in the manner complained is not authorized by the copyright owner, its agent, or the law" and

6. A "statement that the information in the notification is accurate, and under penalty of perjury, that the complaining party is authorized to act on behalf of the owner" of the exclusive right that is being infringed.[63]

Once the registered agent receives notification of the infringement, and he removes the material or blocks the public's access to it, the company is immune from liability for copyright infringement. If he doesn't remove or disable access to the allegedly infringing material, you can seek an injunction against the company to force them to disable access to the allegedly infringing material.

In the event that you forget to include one of the six elements required by the DMCA, your takedown notice could still be valid. In *Brave New Films 501(c)(4) v. Weiner*, the court held that a takedown notice was valid under the DMCA even though it did not include a statement that the complaining party had a good faith belief that the alleged infringer did not have authorization to use the material in the manner complained.[64] The DMCA requires that you "substantially" comply with the takedown notice requirements.

---

63.   17 U.S.C. § 512(c)(3) (2012).

64.   Brave New Films 501(c)(4) v. Weiner, 626 F.Supp.2d 1013, 1017-18 (N.D. Cal. 2009).

The fact that this element was missing was cured by the inclusion of the statement, under penalty of perjury, that the information in the takedown notice was accurate and that the copyrighted material was posted on the Internet without the original author's permission.

It's also possible that your DMCA takedown notice could be invalid if you forget one of the six elements. For example, if you do not give the hosting company enough information to identify and locate the allegedly infringing material on the website, the takedown notice will be invalid.[65] In that situation, the company cannot be held liable for copyright infringement if they do not block the allegedly infringing content because they can't tell which content was supposedly published in violation of your copyright.

If a hosting company does not have a registered agent, check the hosting company's terms of service for information regarding DMCA takedown notices. Some companies do not register an agent with the Copyright Office but state in the terms of service that they will comply with DMCA takedown notices and where to send them. If the company does not have this provision in the website terms of service, you may contact the company directly and ask if the company will comply if you send the company a DMCA takedown notice.

IF SOMEONE SENDS A DMCA TAKEDOWN NOTICE TO YOUR WEB HOST

When a website that hosts others' content receives a DMCA takedown notice, it is required to remove or disable access to the alleged infringing content. It must also take "reasonable steps" to inform the person who posted the material that his content was removed or blocked. If you receive notice from your web host that your content

---

65.   Perfect 10, Inc. v. CCBill, LLC, 340 F.Supp.2d 1077, 1089 (C.D. Cal. 2004).

was removed after it received a DMCA takedown notice, you have three options:

1. You can admit that you copied someone else's work and do nothing.

2. You can accept that someone thinks you copied him when you didn't and do nothing.

3. You can fight back and instruct your web host to restore your content to your site.

You have the right to claim that your work does not constitute copyright infringement.[66] You can have your content put back on your website by sending a DMCA counter notice to the same registered DMCA agent that informed you of the initial takedown notice.

Once the designated agent receives the counter notification, the agent must send a copy of the counter notification to the person who sent the takedown notice and inform him that the removed or blocked material will be restored within ten business days. Your web host must restore the removed or blocked material in ten to fourteen days after receiving the counter notification.[67]

The counter notification, like the takedown notice, must be in writing and include the following:

1. Your physical or electronic signature

2. Identification of the material that was removed or blocked and its URL before it was removed or blocked

3. A "statement under penalty of perjury" that you have "a good faith belief that the material was removed or disabled as a result of mistake or misidentification of the material to be removed or [blocked]"

---

66.   17 U.S.C. § 512(g) (2012).
67.   17 U.S.C. § 512(g)(2) (2012).

4. Your name, address, telephone number, and a statement that you consent to jurisdiction of Federal District Court for the judicial district in which the address is located and that you will accept service of process from the person who sent the initial DMCA takedown notice.[68]

The purpose of the DMCA is to protect websites and hosting companies from being liable for copyright infringement that they did not directly commit. They have an obligation to remove suspected infringing content when they receive a DMCA takedown notice and restore it when they receive a DMCA counter notice. At that point, the person who claims that you are infringing on his work can sue you directly in federal court where he lives. In the notification and counter notification you both stated that you each had a good faith belief regarding the accuracy of your statements, *under the penalty of perjury*. If the court finds that either of you was lying, the liar could face penalties for perjury.

SHOULD YOU REGISTER A DMCA AGENT?

If you allow other people to post content on your site, even if they are only allowed to post comments on your posts, you should consider whether you want to register an agent, so you qualify for DMCA protection under the Copyright Act. If someone posts a comment on one of your blogs that infringes on another person's copyright, the worst-case scenario is that you could be at least partially liable for copyright infringement.

If few people leave comments on your blog, it is unlikely that you will be accused of this type of copyright infringement. If you allow others to post significant amounts of text, photos, or videos on your site; if you allow guest bloggers to create content for you; or if you

---

68.   17 U.S.C. § 512(g)(3) (2012).

receive a lot of comments on your work, it might be worth it to pay the $105 fee to register a DMCA agent.[69] This is particularly true if you do not review others' content before it appears on your site. Having a registered agent could save you from having to pay hundreds if not thousands of dollars in a copyright infringement lawsuit. You should also provide your DMCA agent's contact information on your site's terms of service. If you do not register an agent but would comply with a takedown notice if you receive one, you should state this on your terms of service and the appropriate contact information.

It makes sense to register an agent for DMCA protection if you have multiple contributing writers for your blog. You don't always know if your writers created their content themselves, and you may not take the time and energy needed to verify that their work is original. It's more likely that a person will copy someone else's work on a blog post than in a comment on someone else's blog. You may want to require your writers to sign a contract that indemnifies you against any copyright infringement claims that are made against you or your website because of the guest blogger's work. The contract should state that he will pay for your lawyers' fees and any damages or settlement costs the court orders you to pay.

If you are the only person who writes for your blog and you moderate all the comments before they are posted, it is unlikely that copyright infringement will occur on your site without your knowledge. Under these circumstances, you may not think it's necessary to register a DMCA agent to protect yourself against copyright infringement claims.

BE AWARE OF DMCA ABUSE

One of the problems that has occurred since the DMCA was added to the Copyright Act is some plagiarizers are abusing the law to

---

69. Fees, U.S. Copyright Office, last visited May 31, 2013, http://www.copyright.gov/docs/fees.html.

eliminate their competition. The plagiarizer will copy a blogger's work onto his site and send a DMCA takedown notice to the company that hosts the blogger's website to get the original content removed.[70] The blogger can have their content restored by sending a DMCA counter takedown notice to their web host; however, this will not prevent the plagiarizer from repeating the behavior again. The blogger could sue the plagiarizer for copyright infringement, which may be challenging if the plagiarizer lives outside the country. In that situation, it might be more effective to install software on your blog that prevents readers from right-clicking or copying your content with the Control + C command on their keyboards. If you make it too challenging for someone to steal your work, you can hope that he will move onto someone who hasn't installed this software.

IN SUMMARY

- You can monitor the Internet for potential infringement of your blog's content with Google Alerts or plagiarism software and by regularly checking your site's analytics to see how visitors are getting to your website.

- The DMCA provides an efficient way to address suspected infringement if your goal is to remove your material from others' sites.

- If you allow others to post significant amounts of content on your website, consider registering a DMCA agent with the Copyright Office to protect yourself against infringement claims.

---

70. John Timmer, "Site plagiarizes blog posts, then files DMCA takedown on originals," *ARS Technica*, Feb. 5, 2013, http://arstechnica.com/science/2013/02/site-plagiarizes-blog-posts-then-files-dmca-takedown-on-originals/.

Chapter 6
BLOGGING FOR OTHERS

According to ALM Legal Intelligence, over sixty percent of law firms maintain at least one blog.[71] These law firms must get their blog content from their lawyers, in-house marketing staff, or outside marketing professionals or hiring freelance writers to blog for them. This raises the question of who owns this content.

The Copyright Act has a provision for "works made for hire" that applies to situations where a person is hired to create copyrightable works, and certain commissioned works, as part of his employment.[72] A blog can be a work made for hire in some circumstances.

When your blog post is a work made for hire, you don't own the copyright to your content. Your employer or the person who commissioned it does. You can still get credit for creating the post if the person who hired you decides to give you credit or if your contract requires the attribution, but that's often where your rights end. The person who hired you to create the post will have the exclusive right to decide the circumstances under which it will be published, copied, displayed, or performed, and what derivative works will be made

---

71. Kevin O'Keefe, "4 in 10 law firms report landing new clients through blogging and other social media," *Real Lawyers Have Blogs*, Feb. 29, 2012, http://kevin.lexblog.com/2012/02/29/4-in-10-law-firms-report-landing-new-clients-through-blogging-and-other-social-media/.
72. 17 U.S.C. § 101 (2012).

from it. You cannot use your post in another project, republish the post on your own personal website, or put it in your work portfolio without the owner's permission.

Your blog may be work made for hire if you blog as part of your employment or if you are a freelance blogger for others. If you fall into one of these categories, it's important that you understand when your blogs are works made for hire, and your options to maximize your rights.

BLOGGING AS AN EMPLOYEE

If you are an employee and one of these job responsibilities is to write blogs for the company, every blog post you write for the company is a work made for hire. Your employer is considered the posts' author and owns the copyright to all the content of your work blogs, not you. You may not put any copies of these blog posts in your portfolio to seek other work without your employer's permission. Doing so would infringe on your employer's exclusive rights to decide where its blogs will be reproduced and displayed.

Your employer only obtains the copyright to the exact expression you create for the company. You may write about the same topics in your personal blog or for your portfolio, unless your work contract prohibits this. You just can't copy what you specifically created for your employer without their permission. If you want to use the exact verbiage from a post, you may have to purchase a license to use the work or purchase the copyright outright.

If you have a Twitter handle or accounts on other social media sites that you use to promote the company and its blog, there may be a legal question regarding who owns the accounts and whether you retain the rights to your accounts and your followers when you leave the company. These are issues you and your employer should resolve in writing before you create these accounts. In most cases, when an employee's job includes managing or promoting the company on social media, I suggest the employee have separate social media accounts for employee-related and personal posts. You may promote your employer or its blog on your personal social media accounts; however, your employer cannot require you to promote the company via your personal accounts. That is often a violation of the social media site's terms of services. The company should only promote itself through its own social media accounts.

INDEPENDENT CONTRACTORS

If you are a freelance legal blogger, companies hire you to write blogs on their behalf. You might be hired by a law firm, bar association, legal organization, or company that wants a blog post about a legal topic. Unlike people who blog as company employees, the company that hires you may not automatically own the copyright to the blog posts you create for them. The company will own the content you create for them if you have a written agreement that is signed before you begin the work, if the contract states that your posts are works made for hire, and if your blog posts qualify as "commissioned works." According to the Copyright Act, a commissioned work made for hire must fit into one of the following nine categories:

1. A contribution to a collective work

2. Part of a motion picture or other audiovisual work

3. A translation

4. A supplementary work to a publication (i.e., forward, afterword, illustration, map, chart, table, musical arrangement, bibliography, appendixes, editorial notes)

5. A compilation

6. An instructional text

7. A test

8. Answer materials for a test

9. An atlas

The law regarding works made for hire was obviously created for copyrightable projects that have multiple contributors, such as books and movies. There is a viable argument that blogs created by freelance writers are part of a collective work or a compilation, especially when they will be appearing on a website or in a newsletter or other publication where the other content is created by other writers and artists.

If you blog as an independent contractor and you don't have a contract that was signed before you started blogging stating that your posts are works made for hire, you likely own the copyright to the content you create. The company that hired you does not own it; it just has a license to release it on their website. If you find yourself in this situation, you own all the exclusive copyrights regarding the reproduction, distribution, and display of your posts, and the right to make derivative works based on your content. You can register your copyright with the Copyright Office. If the company wants to use your posts in other ways, it needs your permission to do so. If the company wants to own the copyright to your work, you can make them buy it from you.

There is a counter-argument to the assertion that a blog is a collective work. In Chapter 4, we saw that the Copyright Office declared that blogs did not qualify as collective works. Based on this assessment, blogs may not fit into one of the work made for hire categories. Based on this information, your work as a freelance blogger is not a work made for hire; therefore, you will retain the copyright in your work unless you assign the copyright in writing to the company that hired you. If you do not assign the copyright to the company, the company will have an implied license to release your work on the company's website. If the company repurposes the your content without your permission, you may have a copyright infringement claim against the company for copying and/or creating a derivative work based on your content without your permission.

If the company wished to obtain the copyrights in your work, it would have to purchase it from you.

To avoid these problems, it is best for you and the hiring company to have an agreement that states that your blog posts are works made for hire and that if your work is found not be works made for hire, then you assign the intellectual property rights in the content created under the terms of the agreement to the company.

Additionally, law firms that hire third party bloggers should want assurance that your work is original to you and that you have permission to use any of the images that you submit to accompany blog posts. The law firm should have you sign an agreement that states that you will indemnify the law firm against any infringement claims made against the firm because of your work. This provision should require you to pay any reasonable lawyers' fees and damages assessed against the firm in an intellectual property dispute based on your content.

ARE YOU AN EMPLOYEE OR AN INDEPENDENT CONTRACTOR?

If a court has to decide who owns the copyright to a work, it may start by examining whether you were an employee or an independent contractor when you created the work in question, which may have a significant impact on who owns the copyright to your work. The court will consider how much control the company that hired you had over your work. It may examine many factors in deciding whether you were an employee or an independent contractor including:

- The skill level required to create the work
- Who provided the tools and equipment to create the work
- Where you performed your work
- Whether the company could assign you other tasks
- Whether you worked on an ongoing or on a project basis

- Whether the company could control the days and hours you worked
- Whether you were paid hourly, weekly, or on a project basis
- Whether the company controlled your ability to hire assistants
- Whether the company does the type work that you were hired to perform as part of its business
- Whether you received employee benefits
- How the company classified you in terms of taxes.[73]

The court will consider the totality of circumstances surrounding your employment, not simply the label you or the company uses to classify you.

LICENSING YOUR BLOG CONTENT

When you write blog posts for your own company or blog, you have the ability to license your work to others. When you license your work, you retain the copyright to it, but you give someone permission to use your work for a particular purpose. For example, you may write content that others can repurpose or republish on their websites. If you create original artwork or infographics, you may license it to others to use in their projects.

The benefit of licensing is that it allows you to use the same content in multiple ways. This increases your chance of exposure, as well as your ability to make money multiple times from one literary or artistic work. On the flip side, if you want to license blog material from other bloggers, it might have a negative effect on your search engine optimization (SEO) if the same content is appearing on multiple websites. If you license blog content from others, you may want to get an exclusive license.

---

73. Community for Creative Non-Violence, et al. v. Reid, 490 U.S. 730, 751-52 (1989).

The licensing agreement must be specific about how the person who is licensing your work can use it and whether the license is exclusive or non-exclusive. When you grant someone an exclusive license, only that person can use your content in a particular way. If you give someone an exclusive license to use your content, you may not be able to use your content unless the agreement permits it. When you give someone a non-exclusive license, you have the ability to license the same content to other people to use in similar ways, and to use it yourself.

Be mindful when you write your licensing agreements that you specify how the other person may use your work, including whether he has the ability to sublicense your content to others—including other blogs and publications—and any limits on where your work may appear. You may not be happy if you license your content to someone who shares it on a website you find offensive such as your alma mater's arch rival, an organization whose values and goals you disagree with, or a blog owned by someone that you don't like. You also want to specify how long the license will last—whether the person can use your work forever or only for a limited amount of time. You should also be clear about the payment structure.

It may seem strange that you can create a blog post or other content and not be able to use it, but that's how it is sometimes. If you sell your copyright to someone or you create a work made for hire, you can't use your own work without the risk of being accused of copyright infringement. If you sell your copyright to someone else and you later regret the decision, you can ask to buy it back from whomever owns it. When you create a work made for hire, particularly if you're a freelance blogger, make sure your contract includes a license for you to use the work you create in your portfolio so you can use it as a work sample to obtain other employment. With this license, the other person or company retains ownership of the copyright, but you have permission to use the work in a limited way.

IN SUMMARY

- If you blog as an employee, your employer will be the original author of all your content and own all the copyright rights in your work.

- If you are a contracted legal blogger, the hiring party will not own the copyright in your work unless you have a works made for hire contract that is in writing and signed prior to you doing the work or unless you assign the copyright to him.

- If a court has to determine whether you are an employee or independent contractor, it will consider the totality of the circumstances, not simply what title you and the hiring party use for you.

- When you write your licensing agreements, make sure they address whether the license is exclusive or non-exclusive, the payment terms, whether the licensee may sublicense your work to others, and the duration of the license.

Chapter 7

PROTECTING
CONFIDENTIAL SOURCES

Shield laws are state laws that prevent journalists from having to reveal the identities of anonymous news sources. Journalists in these states are required to disclose a source's identity only when the party requesting the information shows that the information requested is "highly material and relevant, necessary or critical to the maintenance of the claim, and not obtainable from other available sources."[74] The purpose of these laws is to encourage the dissemination of information. Forty states in the United States currently have shield laws.

There are instances when you may wish to protect a source's identity. You may want to blog about a topic and your source will only speak with you or provide a quote if you agree that you will not disclose who he is. You may be approached by someone who has insider information in a situation that you would normally blog about but he may say that he will only reveal what he know if you maintain the strictest of confidence regarding his identity. I have

---

74. Shoen v. Shoen, 48 F.3d 412, 416 (9th Cir. 1995), citing *In re* Petroleum Products Antitrust Litig., 680 F.2d 5, 7 (2d Cir. 1982).

received requests for posts from people who will provide the details of a situation that they believe is worthy of a blog post if I promise not to use their names.

There are ongoing questions regarding whether bloggers qualify as journalists, and are thus protected by state shield laws. Each state that has a shield law has to determine if a blogger can qualify as a journalist and under what circumstances. If you are sued because of your blog and you want to protect a confidential information source, you may have to make an argument that the pertinent state shield law applies to you if this is a matter of first impression. You would likely have to make the argument that you were engaged in the same activities and adhering to the same standards as a traditional journalist in writing your blog, which might convince a court that you should be protected by the shield law.

If you live in a state where oral contracts are binding, you could also argue that revealing your source would violate the terms of the contract. If the court orders you to reveal your information source and you refuse, you could be charged with contempt of court. When working with an anonymous source, you may want to protect yourself by promising to not reveal the source's identity unless ordered to do so by a court of law. It is unlikely that a blogger would create a formal contract with an anonymous source in which the blogger agrees to protect the source's identity in exchange for the source's contribution to a post. However, the terms of a contract could be pieced together if there is a record of text messages or e-mails between the parties discussing their arrangement.

If a court considers you to be the equivalent of a journalist, it will respect your interest in maintaining your source's confidentiality. A judge will order you to disclose a source's identity only if the information is relevant to the case, necessary for the party to present his case, and not available from another source.[75] These are cases where

---

75.   Gonzalez v. National Broad. Co., 194 F.3d 29, 32-33 (2d Cir. 1998). See also People v. Paw-

the court cannot render a fair decision without that information and your informant is possibly the only person who can provide it.

As of this writing (October 2013), the courts in California and New Hampshire have ruled that bloggers are protected by their states' shield laws, and the courts in Oregon and Illinois have ruled that bloggers are not protected by their states' shield laws.[76] The verbiage for each state's shield law is different, and some laws may be worded so narrowly that a court could fairly say that the law cannot apply to bloggers. It is interesting to note that the judge in the Illinois case ruled that bloggers aren't protected by the shield laws in Illinois or California, and this ruling came down after a California court held that bloggers are protected by the California shield law.

From a logical perspective, it seems that a blogger who engages in the same activities as a journalist should have the same protections as a journalist under the shield laws. It also seems logical that courts should not make blanket decisions about whether all bloggers are protected by a shield law, but should evaluate each case on its merits to determine if a particular blogger qualifies for protection. However, many state shield laws require regular publication. Based on that requirement, you may not be protected by a shield law if you publish only sporadically. Additionally, you may not be protected if the definition of "publication" requires a paper printing or applies the same definition of "published" as the Copyright Act. A state shield law may only mention journalists who create content for newspapers, TV, and radio. If that is the case, you would have to convince a judge or jury that the shield law should also extend to electronic publications.

---

laczyk, 724 N.E.2d 901, 908-09 (Ill. 2000).

76. O'Grady v. Superior Court, 44 Cal.Rptr.3d 72, 105 (2006); Mortg. Specialists v. Implode-Explode, 999 A.2d 184, 197 (N.H. 2010); Obsidian Finance Group, LLC v. Cox, Dist. Court, D. Oregon 2012, No. 3:11-cv-57-HZ.; "Judge: Blogger not a reporter, must turn over information," *Chicago Tribune*, Apr. 1, 2012, http://carrollstandard.com/news/crime-and-punishment/verdict/15997-judge-blogger-not-a-reporter-must-turn-over-information.html.

At times you may have to offer someone a promise of anonymity to get information or a quote for your blog. If you ignore or forget about your promise and disclose a source in your blog after promising not to do so in exchange for information, you could face a lawsuit for breach of contract.[77]

The debate over whether bloggers qualify as journalists is not going away any time soon, and since this is a state law issue, we may remain in this situation where some states protect bloggers under the shield law and others do not. Given that blogs are accessible everywhere there's an Internet connection, this issue is likely to get more complicated in the future.

IN SUMMARY

- Shield laws allow journalists to protect their anonymous sources unless their information is critical to maintaining a claim and not otherwise available.
- Shield laws are state laws; therefore whether a blogger is protected by a state's shield law must be determined by each state court. The courts that have ruled on this issue have made discordant rulings.

---

77. Best Western International, Inc. v. Doe, 2006 U.S. Dest. LEXIS 56014 (2006), CV-06-1537-PHX-DGC, October 24, 2006.

Chapter 8
LEGAL RISKS WITH ALLOWING COMMENTS AND GUEST POSTS ON YOUR BLOG

Every blog has the potential to be the beginning of a conversation. Many times the best part of a blog post is the discussion and discourse in the comments that follow a post. Frankly, I don't understand why anyone creates a blog and does not allow comments. There may be the occasional post where you want it to be a stand-alone piece, but in general, if you want to share your thoughts on a blog, you should be open to discussing it further in the comments section.

If you want to make an impact with your blog, draft your blog posts with strong verbiage or take a solid stance on an issue related to the blog's purpose or your practice areas. These posts will stir up your readers' emotions and inspire them to respond with comments. Part of being an effective blogger is to stimulate your audience. And it's OK that they disagree with you sometimes—that's an indicator that you're writing about a topic that matters. Sometimes readers don't disagree with you as much as they disagree with the law. It's also acceptable for you to use your blog to write about issues where the laws don't make sense or need to be updated to accommodate the changing times and circumstances that did not exist when the laws were enacted.

RESPONDING TO BLOG COMMENTS

Part of allowing comments on your blog is a responsibility to respond to them. When you allow comments on your blog posts, it's an invitation to your readers to interact with you and each other. You can't just start the conversation and walk away. When you reply to readers' comments, always be respectful. The reader may misunderstand the purpose or content of a post and may be mollified with a kind response that clarifies the message.

Some people may leave comments on your blog simply to attack you. They might be having a bad day and looking for someone to take it out on, or they may genuinely not like you as a person. Regardless of the reason, it's often OK and even beneficial to allow these comments to appear on your blog if you respond appropriately to them. When you respond to an attack with a calm and professional tone that focuses on the issue and not the person, you look very eloquent and build your reputation for having grace under fire. You can invite the commenter to contact you directly to set up a meeting to discuss his concerns, which shows that you directly address problems and are solution-oriented. This can have a positive impact on your relationship with this commenter and especially on the reputation you are building in the eyes of the other readers who are watching this dialogue unfold.

BENEFITS OF BLOG COMMENTS

There are many benefits that accompany blog comments. They provide an opportunity for your readers to request clarification regarding your posts. Many lawyers use their blogs to write for the needs of their clients and potential clients, and it can be challenging to translate the legalese we use every day into layman's terms. You can use the comments section to help ensure that readers understand your message. Questions from your readers can inspire additional blog posts and ideas for other legal services you may want to offer through your firm. Additionally, some readers comment on blogs to attempt to be heard and validated. When you respond to their comments, you are building a relationship with those individuals and demonstrating to other readers who might be watching that you care about your clients as people, not just about their legal problems.

Allowing comments on your blog also provides an opportunity for other professionals to connect with you. It's a wonderful venue to interact with other professionals who want to know you and your firm better. These interactions could form the beginning of collaborative work relationships or valuable referral sources.

LEGAL RISKS RELATED TO BLOG COMMENTS

There are very few legal issues when it comes to allowing comments on your blog because it's unlikely that you'll be held responsible for other people's statements that are made on your site. Section 230 of the Communication Decency Act states that the owner of a blog "shall not be treated as the publisher or speaker of any information provided by another information content provider."[78] Blog owners are not held civilly liable for defamation, invasion of privacy, or tort claims arising from statements made on a blog by other people. If a comment is particularly offensive or objectionable, you may edit it before allowing it on your site if you do not change the meaning of the message. You may also opt to be cautious and not approve the comment in question if you moderate your blog comments.

When you create a blog, you have the option to moderate your comments or not. When your comments are moderated, a comment

---

78. 47 U.S.C. § 230(c) (2012).

cannot be added to a post without your review and approval. When comments are not moderated, they are added to a post without your advance review. Allowing unmoderated comments increases the chances that spam comments will appear on your website or that offensive comments that you would otherwise disallow would be seen. Moderating comments, gives you more control over what appears on your website and increases the chances that you could be held liable for comments on your website. However, so long as you prevent material that you suspect is illegal, it is doubtful that you will approve a comment that blatantly violates another's rights. In general, I encourage you to allow moderated comments and to review and respond to comments in a timely fashion.

CONSIDER CREATING TERMS OF SERVICE FOR YOUR BLOG

You should also be aware that the terms of service for your website (if you have them) create expectations for your readers. These terms set the ground rules for your relationship with your readers. You can set limits and expectations regarding commenters' statements on your site and create provisions designed to protect your interests. If your terms say that you'll protect the identity of anonymous commenters unless ordered to reveal it by court order, you have an obligation to refuse to release that information until a court orders you to do so. You can have terms that require commenters to post only their own thoughts and not violate anyone's rights with their comments. Your terms can also require commenters to indemnify you and pay any legal fees and penalties you incur as a result of what they post on your blog. You can also create provisions that state you'll respond to any DMCA takedown notices you receive in accordance with the Copyright Act, even if you do not have a registered DMCA agent. Your terms can include a dispute resolution clause that requires people to resolve problems with you in your state under your state's laws, that they have to use the process you state in your terms (mediation, arbitration, or litigation), and pay your lawyers' fees if you are the prevailing party.

LEGAL RISKS WITH GUEST POSTS ON YOUR BLOG

When you have a blog, you may want to invite guest bloggers to contribute posts. A guest blogger can provide a different perspective on a topic or use his expertise to highlight a topic. If your guest writer is well known, you can use his influence to bring more attention to your site. When a guest blogger writes for your website, he will likely promote it among his friends and fans, which will drive traffic to your site and hopefully turn them into fans of your website. Furthermore, writing for your website will be an implied endorsement by the guest blogger for you and your work.

There are significantly more legal issues related to having guest bloggers on your site than allowing comments. You want to make sure your ducks are in a row before you invite others to contribute to your blog.

CREATE A WORK MADE FOR HIRE CONTRACT

When you want to use a guest blogger, the two of you need to determine in advance who will own the copyright to the blog post he creates. Will the guest writer own all the rights and grant you a license to publish his work, or will you own the rights to his work? If you want to own the copyright to your guest blogger's work, you will need a written work-made-for-hire contract signed before the blogger begins his work. If you don't, your guest blogger will likely maintain the copyright to his work, and you will have only an implied license to use his work on your blog.

This is particularly pertinent if you have plans for re-purposing your guest blogger's work in other blog posts or other marketing materials. If you don't own the copyright to his work, you may need his permission and a license to create derivative works based on his original blog post.

You may want to add a term to your work-made-for-hire contract that states that in the event that the project is not work made for hire, the artist assigns all intellectual property rights to the work to you. That will help ensure that you will own the intellectual property right to the work regardless of what the project is or when the contract was signed. It will also be evidence that the intent of the parties was that you would be the owner of work that the guest blogger created.

INDEMNIFY YOURSELF

When you allow guest bloggers to create content for your blog, you want to have a contract in place that indemnifies you of any wrongdoing that might result from publishing their posts. This contract will be an extra layer of protection beyond that afforded by Section 230 of the Communications Decency Act if you are accused of violating anyone's rights by inviting someone to contribute to your blog. You may want to protect yourself against claims of defamation, invasion of privacy, and any type of intellectual property infringement. You also want to make sure your interests are protected in the event that your guest blogger does not use original verbiage, selects images for the post without obtaining the proper permission, or otherwise violates a person's rights in his post.

Depending on the situation, you may not need a contract like this to protect yourself; however, the extra precaution can't hurt you. You may want to include a provision in the contract that states that your guest blogger has to pay for all your lawyers' fees and any damages assessed against you due to any wrongdoing that occurs because of his blog posts.

OTHER CONTRACT PROVISIONS

Some bloggers will contact you and offer to provide blog posts for your website. If you are going to have a marketing company create blog posts for your website or if you are using guest bloggers, you will want a contract that states that their posts will appear only on your website. You want your contract to explicitly state whether you will own the copyright in whatever they create for your website or if you will simply have a license to show the work on your blog. Some marketing companies will write general blog posts and license them to several different websites. If the content from your website matches posts that are on other blogs, it will have a negative effect on your search engine results. You want to make sure you have the exclusive rights to guest posts.

Your contract with your guest blogger or marketing company should also include a dispute resolution provision. Ideally, this contract will require all the parties to resolve any problems in your state and under your state's laws. You can include a provision that requires the parties to resolve their problems via mediation, arbitration, or litigation. Additionally, you may want to add a provision that requires the non-prevailing party to pay the prevailing party's lawyers' fees.

When you're considering inviting guest bloggers to contribute to your site, your focus may be on growing your readership or decreasing your workload, and not on preventing potential legal problems. It's important that you create a framework for yourself so you're protected in case a worst-case scenario happens.

REGISTER A DMCA AGENT WITH THE COPYRIGHT OFFICE

When you write a blog, you know that your work is your own. When you invite someone else to write a guest post for your blog or allow comments on your site, you don't know for certain that the contributors' work is their own. There is always a risk that a guest writer or commenter will rip off someone else's work and pass it off as his own. You can protect yourself by registering a DMCA agent with the Copyright Office. When you register a DMCA agent, you are obliged to take down allegedly infringing material on your website when you receive DMCA takedown notices (see Chapter 5 for more information about DMCA agents).

Registering an agent is cheaper and faster than dealing with a copyright infringement lawsuit. It costs only $105 to register a DMCA agent with the Copyright Office. The minimum fine for copyright infringement is $200 if the court awards the plaintiff statutory damages. Additionally, resolving a copyright infringement lawsuit can take months, if not years, and thousands of dollars in lawyers' fees.

If you allow guest bloggers to write for your blog, you should create terms of service for your website. It should include information about your DMCA agent and how to send DMCA takedown notices. You may want to create a special e-mail address for your DMCA agent, such as DMCA@companyname.com, so the takedown notices won't get lost in your inbox. Additionally, it will ensure that the e-mail address will continue to exist if the person who was initially designated to receive these notices leaves the company.

You may also wish to do this to protect yourself against copyright infringement by commenters.

It's possible, but improbable, that this will occur since most people comment on blogs to leave their own opinions, not to claim someone else's opinion as their own.

If you do not register a DMCA agent with the Copyright Office, you can include a provision in your terms of service that you will remove any allegedly infringing material on your site if you receive a DMCA takedown notice that complies with the DMCA's requirements. Many people do not register an agent but will take down material if they receive a takedown notice about material on their websites. You may not be protected by the DMCA if you do not register a DMCA agent; however, many people who find their work on other websites without their permission are only interested in getting their work removed.

ALTERNATIVE TO GUEST POSTS

While I regularly write guest posts for other blogs, as of this writing (October 2013), I have not allowed anyone to be a guest blogger on my personal blog or my law firm's blog. I don't want to deal with the potential liability that comes with letting others write content for my sites. If there is a person whose perspective I would like to share on one of my blogs, I invite them to do an interview for a post. I only do this when the topic is personal to the interviewee so the chances of them committing infringement or violating someone's rights in their answers are low. I usually do the interview by e-mail so I have a chance to review, edit, and get their approval of my edits before releasing the post. This also allows me to select the questions strategically if necessary, to avoid foreseeable problems and problematic topics.

IN SUMMARY

- Allowing comments on your blog creates a valuable opportunity for readers to interact with you and each other.

- The Communications Decency Act states that you will not be held liable if a commenter or guest blogger commits defamation, invasion of privacy, or another tort with what they post on your blog.

- If you allow guest bloggers on your site, write an effective contract that addresses potential intellectual property and civil claims that could result from their posts.

- Consider registering a DMCA agent to protect yourself against copyright claims for what commenters and guest bloggers post on your blog.

Chapter 9

DEFAMATION

One of the benefits of having a blog is the ability to share potentially scandalous information and breaking news. While it's fun to share these stories, be careful that you don't inadvertently defame someone in the process. In most cases, defamation occurs because of an innocent slip or a forgotten but pertinent piece of information that changes the whole story.[79] The First Amendment protects your freedom of speech, but it does not protect defamatory speech.[80]

Defamation is the basis for a civil lawsuit where the plaintiff claims the defendant made a false statement about the plaintiff to a third party, damaging the plaintiff's reputation.[81] Publishing a defamatory statement on your blog qualifies as a communication to a third party, even if your readership is negligible or nonexistent. You can be sued for damaging the reputation of an individual or a company.

---

79. David Bodney, "10 Misconceptions About Libel Law," *Editor & Publisher*, Vol. 130 Issue 25, p. 90, Jun. 21, 1997.
80. Doe v. Cahill, 884 A.2d 451, 456 (Del. 2005).
81. *Black's Law Dictionary* (9th ed. 2009); L. Eldredge, Law of Defamation 5 (1978).

There are two types of defamation: libel and slander. Libel is a written defamatory statement. Slander is a spoken defamatory statement. Each state has its own laws regarding defamation; this chapter provides only general information. You should look up the applicable law for your situation.

When you write blog posts, be mindful of what information sources you use. If you repeat another person's defamatory statement, you may be held responsible as the person who made the original defamatory statement.[82] The Communications Decency Act may also protect you in these situations if you repeat defamatory information that you obtained from "another information content provider."[83] If you provide the facts on which your conclusion was based, but your facts are incorrect or incomplete, you could also be accused of defamation.[84]

You need to be deliberate about your word selection. You can be sued for defamation if you accuse someone of a crime he has not committed. Be cautious if you have the impulse to describe someone as a killer, thief, or rapist if your readers might interpret your description as a fact rather than rhetorical hyperbole.[85] If you want to discuss an ongoing criminal investigation or case, it's important to use words like *alleged* and *accused* until the defendant is convicted. Moreover, adding the phrase *in my opinion* to any statement that would otherwise be read as a fact will not protect you in a defamation case.[86] Many courts will rule it's just as bad to say "In my opinion, my neighbor's a pedophile" as "My neighbor's a pedophile" if you cannot prove that your neighbor is in fact a pedophile.

As a legal blogger, you need to be concerned about avoiding making defamatory statements in your posts and comments. As we

---

82. Bodney, *supra* note 80.
83. 47 U.S.C. § 230 (c)(1) (2012).
84. Milkovich v. Lorain Journal Co., 497 U.S. 1, 18–19 (1990).
85. Greenbelt Cooperative Publishing Ass'n, Inc. v. Bressler, 398 U.S. 6, 13–14 (1970).
86. Milkovich at 18–19.

saw in Chapter 8, you generally won't have control over what others post on your website. The law will hold you responsible for your statements and the statements you direct others to make; otherwise, the Communications Decency Act will hold you immune from penalty for defamation committed by others on your blog.[87]

Conversely, your opinions about a situation are not defamatory as long as you don't say anything that would be interpreted as a factual statement. Your emotional reactions to an event and your first-hand observations are generally not defamation. You might be accused of defamation if you call a defendant a sociopath, but you are likely OK if you write, "I get a weird vibe when I see the defendant's icy stare in the courtroom," as long as every part of your statement is true or rhetorical hyperbole. You may still be sued for defamation and have to defend yourself, but you are less likely to lose.

The same rule also applies to your experiences with, and opinions about, companies. You can write a blog to express your dissatisfaction with a company's business practices and invite others to share their experiences. You can encourage your readers to report the company to the proper authority for their wrongdoings as long as your statements are true.[88]

Likewise you may be the target of negative reviews from former clients on websites like Avvo and Yelp. As long as the person is only sharing his opinion about you, there is little you can do about it beyond damage control. However, you may pursue a claim for defamation against someone who writes a review against you that contains a lie. William Gwire is a California lawyer who is doing just that. He is suing former client, Elliot Blumberg, after Blumberg left a review of Gwire that stated Gwire "committed a horrific fraud against me."[89] Fraud is a crime in California; therefore, Gwire may

---

87.   47 U.S.C. § 230 (c)(2) (2012).

88.   Sedgwick Claims Management Services, Inc. v. Delsman, 2009 WL 2157573, *1 (N.D.Cal. 2009).

89.   Stephanie Rabiner, "Attorney Sues Client Over Bad Internet Review," *Strategist*, Nov. 22, 2011,

prevail if he did not commit fraud against his former client. As of this writing (October 2013), the case is still proceeding in Superior Court of California.

If you suspect you've been defamed on someone's blog, the only person you can likely successfully sue is the person who made the defamatory statement. You can't sue the person who owns the website domain where the defamatory statement was published if that person did not make the statement in question.[90] One of the challenges in a case like this might be proving the defendant made the statement against you.

If you are defamed on a website that is owned by an individual or a company that has others create content for its site, you can file a lawsuit for defamation against both the person who defamed you and the website owner who had control over what was published. In that case, the writer may be acting as the agent of the website's owner, which could make both parties liable for defamation.

DEFAMATION CASES INVOLVING ANONYMOUS PERSONS

You may choose to blog anonymously or use pseudonyms to hide your identity. If someone believes he has been defamed by you, he can file a lawsuit against "John Doe" and ask the court to issue a subpoena to the company that hosts your website to learn your identity. When deciding whether to issue the requested subpoena, the court will weigh the alleged victim's ability to prove defamation has occurred against your First Amendment right to speak anonymously.[91] The alleged victim will have to prove that you made a

---

http://blogs.findlaw.com/strategist/2011/11/attorney-sues-client-over-bad-Internet-review.html.

90.   Kruska v. Perverted Justice Foundation, Inc., 2009 WL 321146, *1 (D.Ariz. 2009); N. Am. Bushman, Inc. v. Saari, 2009 WL 211932, *4-*5 (M.D.Pa. 2009).

91.   Solers v. Doe, 977 A.2d 941, 948, 952 (D.C.Ct.App. 2009), citing Oparaugo v. Watts, 884 A.2d 63, 76 (D.C. 2005) (quoting Crowley v. N. Am. Telecomms. Ass'n, 691 A.2d 1169, 1173 n. 2 (D.C. 1997).

defamatory statement about him to a third party, that you acted, if not maliciously, at least negligently by publishing the statement, and that he has suffered harm as a result. The court will grant the subpoena only if it appears the request was made in good faith, the information is necessary to the case, and if the information is not available from another source.[92]

The company that hosts your blog may try to have the subpoena quashed to avoid releasing your identity. If the company has a policy that states that it will only release anonymous posters' information in response to a court order, the company can fight for its users' First Amendment rights to speak anonymously.[93]

If you blog anonymously or use a pseudonym and you defame someone, you may lose your ability to remain anonymous. If you are sued for defamation, the court may require the company that hosts your site to disclose your name. You may not know that you're being sued for defamation because the person can only sue "John Doe" until he obtains your identity from the company that hosts your site.

If you learn about the lawsuit, you can attempt to protect your right to remain anonymous by filing a writ of mandamus.[94] This gives you the ability to remain anonymous and have an advocate in the courtroom fighting for your right to remain anonymous instead of relying on the company's lawyers to advocate on your behalf. You can also file a motion to seal and ask the court to allow you to represent yourself while maintaining your anonymity. The court will decide whether the company will have to release your personal information. If a court decides that you have defamed the plaintiff, you will be required to pay damages to the party whose reputation you harmed.

---

92. McVicker v. King, 266 F.R.D. 92, 93 (W.D.Pa. 2010).

93. McVicker at 93; Cahill at 460; Independent Newspapers, Inc. v. Brodie, 966 A.2d 432, 445–46 (Md. 2009).

94. *In re* Does 1-10, 242 S.W.3d 805, 810 (Tex. App. 2007).

PUBLIC VS. PRIVATE PERSONS

The court applies different standards to defamation of a public person and defamation of a private person. Public persons are public officials and celebrities who seek the public spotlight. It also includes elected judges and state attorneys general. A private person can become a public figure by "voluntarily injecting (himself) into a limited range of public issues."[95] He will only be considered a public figure for those limited issues. For example, a person who engages in criminal conduct is not automatically a public person,[96] but he may be one in regard to his crimes. Likewise, a lawyer in a high-profile case may be classified as a public person in regard to the trial. A famous or infamous blogger, similar to a book author or columnist, could also become a public person if he becomes well known.

The line distinguishing a public figure from a private person is fuzzy at best. If the parties in a defamation case cannot agree on whether the plaintiff is a private or public person, the court will make that determination. When there is such a dispute, the court usually characterizes the plaintiff as a private person.[97]

DEFAMATION OF A PUBLIC PERSON

When a public person sues for defamation, he cannot win his case unless he proves the defamatory statement was made with "actual malice." He must prove that the writer or speaker knew the statement was false when he made it or that he made the statement with "reckless disregard of the truth."[98]

---

95.   Scottsdale Publishing, Inc. v. Superior Court, 764 P.2d 1131, 1138 (Ariz. Ct. App. 1988), quoting Gertz v. Robert Welch, Inc. 418 U.S. 323, 351 (1974), internal quote omitted.

96.   Wolston v. Readers Digest Ass'n, 4434 U.S. 157, 168 (1979).

97.   Bodney, *supra* note 80.

98.   New York Times Co. at 279–80.

Making a statement with reckless disregard of the truth means the person could have easily determined what the truth was in the situation, such as if he ran a simple Internet search. Proof of "reckless disregard" requires "sufficient evidence to permit the conclusion that the defendant in fact entertained serious doubts as to the truth of his publication."[99] No writer or speaker is going to willingly admit that he "entertained serious doubts as to the truth of the statement," so the court may infer whether he had such doubts.[100]

Determining whether a person acted with actual malice is subjective.[101] You can be accused of acting with actual malice if evidence shows you failed to investigate the veracity of your facts.[102] You may also be accused of malice if you ignore requests for retraction when they are accompanied by specific facts that rebut your inaccurate statements.[103]

DEFAMATION OF A PRIVATE PERSON

There are two categories of defamation of private persons: defamation regarding a matter of public concern and defamation not about a matter of public concern. Matters of public concern are events and issues in which the public has a vested interest, such as crimes in the community and public safety issues. When the statement in question is a matter of public concern, courts are more forgiving of misstatements because the law generally supports the dissemination of information that is pertinent to the public.

When a private person has been defamed, he can ask the court for compensatory and punitive damages. Compensatory damages are meant to make the injured person whole again. Money may not

---

99. St. Amant v. Thompson, 390 .S. 727, 731–32 (1968).
100. Selby v. Savard, 655 P.2d 342, 345 (Ariz. 1982), quoting St. Amant at 731.
101. Dombey v. Phoenix Newspapers, Inc., 724 P.2d 562, 575 (Ariz. 1986).
102. *Id.* at 573.
103. *Id.* at 575.

be able to undo the damage that was done to the person's reputation; however, it gives him the financial benefit he allegedly lost because of the defamatory statement. The purpose of punitive damages is to punish the person who harmed you in addition to making him pay for the damage he caused. Public persons who file defamation lawsuits are only eligible to receive compensatory damages.

When a private person sues for defamation and the statement is a matter of public concern, he can collect compensatory and punitive damages only if he can prove that the statement was made with actual malice. (That's the same standard as for a public person.)[104] The plaintiff can win the case if he can show that the statement was false and it damaged his reputation.[105]

When the allegedly defamed person is a private person and the statement in question is not a matter of public concern, the plaintiff may collect compensatory and punitive damages if he can prove that the statement was false. He is not required to show that the statement was published with malice.[106]

DEFAMATION DEFENSES

Being sued for defamation does not mean that you are going to lose. There are five arguments you can use to dispute a defamation claim:

1. The statement was true.

2. The statement was substantially true.

3. No one would believe that the statement in question was asserting a fact.

4. There was no malice.

5. There was no reputational damage.

---

104. Gertz at 332; Dun & Bradstreet, Inc. v. Greenmoss Builders, Inc., 472 U.S. 749, 753 (1985).

105. Philadelphia Newspapers, Inc. v. Hepps, 475 U.S. 767, 777 (1986).

106. Gertz at 345-346.

Let's examine each potential defense.

DEFENSE 1: THE STATEMENT WAS TRUE.

Defamation requires a false statement; therefore, there can be no defamation if your statement was true. One of the best ways to present accurate information and avoid being accused of defamation is to use "original source material as much as possible."[107]

Public records are a reliable place to find original source material. If you're going to use public records for information, be sure you accurately present the information.[108] If you take a public record out of context or manipulate the truth to communicate the message you want to convey, you may open yourself to a defamation lawsuit.

You should also be careful when you quote another publication. If you quote someone on your blog and that statement turns out to be defamatory, you could be held equally liable as the person who made the false statement.

The downside of relying on the truth as your defense to a defamation claim is that it "is often time-consuming, painful, and expensive."[109] You may have to endure a full court trial before you win the case. If you have to go through a trial, you will have the burden of proving the statement you made was true when you made it.

DEFENSE 2:
THE STATEMENT WAS "SUBSTANTIALLY TRUE."

A court will not find you liable for defamation if your statement was "substantially true," meaning that it was false only in terms of minor

---

107. Bodney, *supra* note 80.
108. *Id.*
109. *Id.*

insignificant details.[110] The court will find that slight inaccuracies are immaterial if the statement was "true in substance."[111]

For example, let's say you saw your neighbor run over a child and drive off into the night. If you write a blog post that says, "I saw my neighbor Bob Jones hit a child with his black car and drive off into the night" and Bob's car is actually dark green, he might sue you for defamation because technically you told a lie about him. Bob will lose the case if the statement was true, except in regards to the color of his car. Your statement will be classified as substantially true if the court says it differs from the truth "only in insignificant details."[112]

DEFENSE 3: NO ONE WOULD BELIEVE THAT THE STATEMENT IN QUESTION WAS ASSERTING A FACT.

If the allegedly defamatory statement was part of a sarcastic, rhetorical, or comedic piece, you could defend yourself by arguing that your statement could not "reasonably [be] interpreted as stating actual facts."[113] There can be no defamation if no reasonable person would believe that your statement was true.

DEFENSE 4: THERE WAS NO MALICE.

If a public person sues you for defamation, that person must prove that you made the false statement with actual malice. You can defend yourself by arguing that there was no actual malice behind your statement. If the plaintiff cannot prove that you knew the statement

---

110. Read v. Phoenix Newspapers, Inc., 819 P.2d 939, 941 (Ariz. 1991).

111. Currier at 1354, quoting Restatement (Second) of Torts § 581(A), comment f (1977).

112. Currier at 1354, quoting Zerangue v. TSP Newspapers, Inc. 814 F.2d 1066, 1073 (5th Cir. 1987).

113. Bresler at 22–23; Hustler Magazine, Inc. v. Falwell, 485 U.S. 46, 50 (1988).

was false or that you should have known that the statement was false, you will not be liable for damaging his reputation.[114]

DEFENSE 5:
THERE WAS NO REPUTATIONAL DAMAGE.

The plaintiff has the burden of proving the false statement damaged his reputation. This is often presented as lost business or other indicators that show a decrease in the person's popularity or credibility. If you made a false statement, but it did not damage the plaintiff's reputation, there is no defamation. This is a hard argument to win because there are many things a plaintiff can do to show reputational damage.

This defense is referred to as the "libel-proof plaintiff doctrine."[115] Essentially, you have to argue that the plaintiff's reputation was so bad that there's nothing you could say that would make it any worse. To win a case using this defense, you have to show that the plaintiff is "incapable of being defamed."[116] This defense is the least likely of all the defamation defenses to be effective.

There is nothing wrong with using strong language in your posts or writing about controversial topics; but you should make sure that all your statements are accurate and use reliable sources for your information. Your feelings and observations of public events are generally protected. Be careful, when you're being judgmental in your posts, that you don't inadvertently cross the line between sharing an opinion and stating a fact.

---

114. Scottsdale Publishing at 1133, citing Dun & Bradstreet, Inc. at 775.
115. Note: "The Libel-Proof Plaintiff Doctrine," 98 Harv.L.Rev. 1909 (1985).
116. Scottsdale Publishing at 1131.

IN SUMMARY

- You may commit defamation if you make a false statement on your blog about a third party that damages the third party's reputation.
- Be deliberate with your word choices. The law cares about what you actually said, not what you meant.
- If you are an anonymous blogger and you defame someone, the court may order your hosting company to reveal your identity for the purpose of the lawsuit.
- The court applies different standards for defamation involving public persons and private persons. A public person must prove that you maliciously or recklessly lied about him.
- You can defend yourself against a defamation claim by showing that the statement in question was true or substantially true, that one would believe the statement asserted a fact, that there was no malice, or that there was no reputational damage.

Chapter 10

INVASION OF PRIVACY AND INTENTIONAL INFLICTION OF EMOTIONAL DISTRESS

Courts respect the idea that people generally have the right "to be let alone."[117] Technological advances such as the global positioning system (GPS), video surveillance cameras, and smart phones have taken away some of that privacy; however, the law still protects confidential relationships and information that you do not share with the public. Each state has its own laws for invasion of privacy and intentional infliction of emotional distress. This chapter provides only general information about these topics. You should look up the laws that apply to your situation.

A person has no expectation of privacy regarding anything he says or does in public. Therefore, you can generally blog about anything that you see or hear in public as long as you're not using things like listening bugs and hidden cameras to obtain your information. Additionally, it is permissible for a lawyer to blog about information

---

117. Samuel D. Warren and Louis D. Brandeis, "The Right to Privacy," 4 Harv.L.Rev. 193 (1890).

about their cases as long as he only uses information that has become public or he obtains his clients' consent.

If you are sued for invasion of privacy, the plaintiff will claim that your blog caused him mental or emotional harm.[118] When you are sued for invasion of privacy, you are essentially being sued for hurting the plaintiff's feelings. This is different from lawsuits for defamation where the plaintiff can only sue you for damaging his reputation.[119]

Only individuals can sue you for invasion of privacy. A company can never successfully sue you for invasion of privacy because it does not have feelings and cannot suffer emotional harm. On the other hand, you can be sued by a person or a company for defamation because they both have reputations that can be damaged.

A person can file a civil lawsuit for invasion of privacy based on the following premises:

- False light
- Public disclosure of private information
- Intrusion upon seclusion
- Misappropriation or commercialization[120]

INVASION OF PRIVACY— FALSE LIGHT

False light invasion of privacy protects against "knowingly or recklessly publishing false information or innuendo that a reasonable person would find highly offensive."[121] A person might sue you for false light if you misrepresent the person's "character, history,

---

118. Reed v. Real Detective Publishing Co., 162 P.2d 133, 139 (Ariz. 1945).
119. Time, Inc. v. Hill, 385 U.S. 374, 384 n. 9 (1967).
120. William L. Prosser, Privacy, 48 Calif.L.Rev. 383 (1960); Restatement (Second) of Torts § 652A-I (1977).
121. Godbehere v. Phoenix Newspapers, Inc., 783 P.2d 781, 786 (1989).

activities or beliefs," in a significant way.[122] A person can win a lawsuit for false light invasion of privacy by proving that you published the information when you knew that it was false or that you published it with a reckless disregard of the truth.

For example, you might write a blog post about your concerns that local drug addicts are selling their blood at plasma centers to fund their drug habits. You might go to the plasma center and take a picture of the building to go with your post. If there are any pedestrians on the sidewalk in your picture, it could suggest that they were people who used the plasma center to fund their drug habits. If a person in the picture was not a drug addict, he might have grounds to sue you for false light. It was true that he was present on the sidewalk when the picture was taken; however, pairing the picture with the blog post misrepresents his activities.

Public persons have put themselves into the public spotlight and can expect criticism and the occasional inaccurate statement. Public officials in particular can expect to have their job performances criticized. The court has ruled that public officials can expect misstatements to occur and thus public officials cannot sue for false light invasion of privacy for matters involving official acts or duties.[123] If a public official sues you for false light invasion of privacy regarding a private matter, he must prove that you acted with actual malice, the same standard as for defamation.[124] This may protect you in situations if you want to write a critical post about a judge or other elected person in the legal profession. (However, you also want to be careful that you don't open yourself up to a bar complaint for being disrespectful to the court.)

If you ever want to sue someone for defamation, you should always include a claim for false light invasion of privacy as well. If

---

122. Godbehere at 787, quoting Restatement (Second) of Torts § 652E, comment c (1977).
123. Godbehere at 789.
124. Restatement (Second) of Torts § 652E, comment b (1977).

you lose on the defamation claim because the court decides that the statement was true, you still have an opportunity to be compensated for your damages based on false light.

INVASION OF PRIVACY— PUBLIC DISCLOSURE OF PRIVATE FACTS

To have a valid claim for public disclosure of private facts, there must be a widespread dissemination of factually accurate information that would normally be confidential and such a disclosure would be highly offensive to a reasonable person.[125] This could occur in a situation where you break up with your significant other and you publish a blog post disclosing all of his secrets, fetishes, and phobias that he would never share with anyone except a romantic partner. The same is true when it comes to posting intimate videos and photos of your former partner. Be careful that you don't post information about family and friends that they shared with you in confidence as it could lead to a lawsuit for public disclosure of private facts.

INVASION OF PRIVACY— INTRUSION INTO SECLUSION

To prove intrusion into seclusion, the plaintiff must have a reasonable expectation of privacy and prove that an intrusion into a private place, conversation, or matter occurred in a manner that is highly offensive to a reasonable person.[126] This could apply to situations where you write a blog about a person that includes information obtained using hidden cameras, microphones, and/or transmitters.

---

125. Godbehere at 786, citing Time, Inc. v. Hill, 385 U.S. 374 (1967); quoting Restatement (Second) of Torts § 652E, comment c (1977).
126. Shulman v. Group W. Prods., Inc., 955 P.2d 469, 490 (Cal. Sup. Ct. 1998).

There can be no intrusion into seclusion claims brought in relation to anything a person does in public because there he has no expectation of privacy. The exceptions to this rule are public places where a person has an expectation of privacy like public bathrooms, changing rooms, and doctors' offices. The exceptions also include confidential meetings between a lawyer and his client. If you violate your client's lawyer-client privilege via your blog, you may face a civil lawsuit as well as a bar complaint.

It may be possible to bring a claim for invasion of privacy for information that was obtained from a workplace. If a person works in an environment that involves intimate information or activities, and information regarding those activities is published, the person could have grounds to bring a claim for intrusion into seclusion.[127] The court held that these work environments are not public so there is an increased expectation of privacy. This does not likely apply to everyday chit-chat around the water cooler, but rather things like information about clients, how your feel a case is going, and your strategy for resolving a client's problem.

INVASION OF PRIVACY— MISAPPROPRIATION OR COMMERCIALIZATION

You have the right to control whether others make money from pictures or video of you. If a company wants to put your face on its product, the company has to obtain your permission to use the image of your face for commercial purposes. Likewise, if you use someone's image for commercial purposes on your blog, you could be sued for commercializing his image without permission.

---

127. Medical Lab Management Consultants v. Am. Broad. Cos., 30 F.Supp.2d 1182, 1188 (D. Ariz. 1998).

This could be a gray area. If you have a financially successful blog and you use a picture of someone who did not consent to the use of his image, he may sue you for commercialization. If the blog post in question was newsworthy, you could make the argument that your blog should be treated like any newspaper or broadcast. In that case you're disseminating news information, not commercializing the person's image. You can avoid this problem by selecting images that do not feature any person or at least no one's face or any identifiable features.

Likewise, if you make money directly from your blog, you may face a claim that blogging about your client, even information that was shared in open court, was a commercialization of their image or their story. This problem can be avoided by obtaining the client's permission to blog about them prior to releasing any posts about the case.

INTENTIONAL INFLICTION OF EMOTIONAL DISTRESS

If a private person feels he has been harmed by a blog post, he may also sue you for intentional infliction of emotional distress. To win such a case, he will have to prove three things:

1. Your conduct was extreme and outrageous.

2. You intended to cause emotional distress, or you recklessly disregarded the near certainty that such distress would occur.

3. He experienced severe emotional distress as a result of your blog post.[128]

It is unlikely that a plaintiff will be successful in this lawsuit, but he can try, and there is a possibility that he will win. A typical blog post, even one with inflammatory content, will not be severe enough to constitute extreme and outrageous conduct.

---

128. Ford v. Revlon, Inc., 734 P.2d 580, 585 (Ariz. 1987); Restatement (Second) of Torts § 46 (1965).

If a public person sues you for intentional infliction of emotional distress, he must prove that you acted with actual malice in addition to proving the three factors listed above.[129] The court applies the same standard as for defamation to determine whether you acted with actual malice.

You should be diligent about publishing only the truth on your blog and being aware of when you might be invading your subject's privacy or causing him emotional harm. Be cognizant of when your blog subjects have an expectation of privacy and do not use hidden cameras or listening devices to obtain your information. Make sure you don't write about anything that you learned in confidence. Be respectful of your clients and put yourself in their shoes before you release any blog posts about their cases. You could damage your relationship with them and lose their trust, which could have a negative impact on the firm and your ability to inspire confidence in your clients, current and potential.

IN SUMMARY

- In general, you can blog about anything you plainly observe in public because a person has no expectation of privacy in that situation.

- Invasion of privacy lawsuits can be based on claims such as false light, public disclosure of private information, intrusion upon seclusion, misappropriation, or commercialization.

- You could commit intentional infliction of emotional distress with your blog if the alleged victim can show your conduct was extreme and outrageous, that you intended to cause emotional distress or recklessly disregarded the near certainty that distress would occur, and he experienced severe emotional distress as a result.

---

129. Falwell at 56.

Chapter 11

BLOGGING AND TRADEMARK LAW

Most people associate trademarks with product labels, slogans, and logos. They don't consider the possibility that they might have trademark rights or problems when they're creating their blogs. You should be aware of the possibility that you might have trademark rights in your blog, opportunities to expand your trademark protection, and potential problems if you are accused of violating someone else's trademark with your blog.

WHAT'S A TRADEMARK?

Trademarks and service marks differentiate your goods and services from others' goods and services. A trademark is any "word, phrase, symbol or design, or a combination thereof, that identifies and distinguishes the source of the goods of one party from those of others."[130] A service mark is mark that "identifies and distinguishes

---

130. U.S. Patent and Trademark Office, Frequently Asked Questions about Trademarks, last visited June 3, 2013, http://www.uspto.gov/faq/trademarks.jsp#_Toc275426672.

the source of a service rather than goods."[131] Most people use the term "trademark" to refer to both trademarks and service marks, so I will too, to avoid confusion. You should be aware that there is a difference between trademarks and service marks, but the law applies equally to both of them.

Trademarks are the marks you put on your goods and services to differentiate them from your competition. They are words like *Nike* and logos like the Nike swoosh. The name and logo for your law firm and/or the firm's blog could be your trademarks. If you have a personal blog, the name of your blog could be your trademark as well as the blog's logo and tagline if you have them. Your domain name could also be a trademark. The purpose of your marks is to inform your readers about the source and qualities of your business and blog compared to others'.

SCOPE OF TRADEMARK PROTECTION

If you don't register your trademark with the United States Patent and Trademark Office (USPTO), you get the exclusive right to use your trademark only in the geographic area where you use it in commerce under the common law. If you have a store, and you didn't register your name with the USPTO, you might only be eligible for trademark protection where people know about your store, which may be your county or possibly your entire state. You might not be able to stop someone from opening a similar store with the same name across the country, unless your trademark is known nationwide.

You obtain protection in your trademark by using it in commerce. Designing and building the blog's website is likely not enough to establish a use in commerce. You must be actively blogging to obtain protection. You may file an Intent To Use application with the USPTO up to six months prior to using your desired mark to

---

131. *Id.*

establish your intention to claim a name, logo, or other mark as your trademark.

If you register your trademark with the USPTO, you get the exclusive national rights to use your mark on your goods and services. No one can begin using your mark on similar goods or services anywhere in the country once you have registered your mark. If someone tries, you can force them to stop using the mark by sending a cease-and-desist letter, or by suing them for trademark infringement and unfair competition.

There is a possibility that you could have competitors who are using a mark that is similar to yours when you register your mark. If that happens, those competitors can keep using their marks as long as they were using them before you registered your mark. Once your mark is registered, your competition becomes "frozen" in their geographic areas where their markets are established. They cannot expand their business beyond their established areas. Likewise, you can't use your mark in their established areas. You can use your mark anywhere else in the country except in these geographic areas where your competition has earned the exclusive right to use that mark.

Here's an example of this phenomena. The first Burger King was an independently owned restaurant in Mattoon, Illinois. The owners didn't register their trademark with the USPTO. After this Burger King opened, the Burger King franchise was created, and they registered "Burger King" as a trademark with the USPTO. The original Burger King was allowed to continue to exist, but it cannot expand beyond its established market, which is a twenty-mile radius around the restaurant. Burger King franchises can be everywhere else in the United States except for in the twenty-mile bubble around the original Burger King.[132]

---

132. Trademark Case Law, IP Legal Services, last visited June 5, 2013, http://www.ipprocurement. com/trademarks/articles/trademark_case_law.html.

These situations can become more complicated in the blogosphere where it is more difficult to establish your geographic market. Turner Barr found himself in such a predicament. He started a blog called Around the World in Eighty Jobs where he blogged and posted videos about his travels around the world, where he worked various jobs to pay for his adventures.[133] His trademark problems started when a marketing company registered the mark "Around the World in Eighty Jobs" for a contest for their client, Adecco, where the winners would travel, work, and blog about their experiences.[134] Barr had common law trademark rights for "Around the World in Eighty Jobs;" however, since his business only existed on the Internet, it was difficult to determine his established market and his blog was essentially shut down.[135] Thankfully for Barr, Adecco gave up their rights to the mark when they were made aware of the situation, apologized to Barr, and paid him $50,000 for his troubles.[136]

Ideally, you should do a trademark search on the USPTO website for the name or logo you want to use before you create your blog.[137] If you pick a name for your blog that is confusingly similar to someone's registered trademark or a trademark that is so well-known it's protected nationwide, they can force you to change your blog's name or logo by sending you a cease-and-desist letter, or by suing you for trademark infringement. Unlike copyright law, there is no fair use defense when it comes to trademarks. It's better to select

---

133. *Around the World in 80 Jobs*, last visited October 23, 2013, http://www.aroundtheworldin80jobs.com/.

134. Turner Barr, "How I Got Fired from a Job I Invented," Around the World in 80 Jobs, June 20, 2013, http://www.aroundtheworldin80jobs.com/how-i-got-fired-from-the-job-i-invented/.

135. Turner Barr, "Even Multi-Billion Dollar Corporations Should Apologize When They Are Wrong: An Open Letter to Adecco to #makeitright," *Around the World in 80 Jobs*, June 24, 2013, http://www.aroundtheworldin80jobs.com/even-multibillion-dollar-corporations-should-apologize-when-they-are-wrong/.

136. Turner Barr, "How to Make it Right in a 2.0 World," *Around the World in 80 Jobs*, June 26, 2013, http://www.aroundtheworldin80jobs.com/how-to-make-it-right-in-a-2-0-world/

137. U.S. Patent and Trademark Office, Trademark Electronic Search System (TESS), last visited July 25, 2013, http://tess2.uspto.gov/.

a name or logo that you know no one has registered or is not confusingly similar to an existing trademark than to put time, energy, and money into rebranding your website.

WHAT'S THE DIFFERENCE BETWEEN TM AND ®?

When you've decided what name, logo, or slogan you want to use as your mark, it's best to put "TM" next to it, usually in superscript. This puts your competition on notice that you are claiming the name, logo, or slogan as the mark that distinguishes your goods or services from others. If you are ever in a trademark dispute, having the "TM" next to what you claim as your mark could be used as evidence of what you claim is your mark and that your competition had notice that you were using a particular mark first.

Once you register your mark with the USPTO, you may change the "TM" to ®. The ® informs everyone that the mark has been registered.

HOW TO REGISTER A TRADEMARK

You can apply to register your mark with the USPTO by submitting an application and paying a fee. Your application has to state what you're claiming as your mark, when you started using it, and on what products or services you're using it. For most blogs, your class of goods or services will be some type of publication or information service. You will be required to pay a separate fee for each class of goods or services for which you are registering your mark. If you're claiming multiple marks, each one will need a separate application.

It may take months to complete the process to register your mark. It will take several weeks for the USPTO to get to your application because of its backlog, and then you may go through a series of inquiries from the USPTO lawyer assigned to review your file. If the USPTO accepts your application, your mark will be published on the USPTO's official gazette where anyone can see it and they have thirty days to object that your mark infringes on their mark. If no one objects, your mark will be registered.

Once you have your mark, you must continue to use it. If you do not use your mark for three consecutive years, your mark will be considered abandoned, and anyone else can use it without penalty. You must periodically file affidavits with the USPTO that state that you're still using your mark. You must file an affidavit between your fifth and sixth year of using the mark, between the ninth and tenth year of using the mark, and every ten years after that.

Each affidavit must state the following:

- What mark is being used
- The goods or services it's being used on
- Any good or service on which you're no longer using your mark

You must also provide samples of your mark as you're using it. A screenshot of your blog should be sufficient.

TRADEMARK PROBLEMS RELATED TO BLOGS

There are two potential problems related to trademarks and your blog. If your blog focuses on your opinions or experiences related to an existing product or service, the company that sells it may claim that you're infringing on its trademark. The other problem you might face is you might be accused of trademark infringement if your name, logo, or slogan for your site is similar to someone else's.

You need to examine the name, logo, overall appearance, and domain for your blog to see if someone might accuse you of copying his established trademark and riding his coattails for your own benefit. If you have a blog that focuses on a particular product, you have to be careful that you don't give the impression that you're trying to represent the company itself.

For example, Don Burnside loves MINI Cooper cars and writes a blog about them.[138] He also has a podcast where he talks about MINI Coopers.[139] If you look at his sites, you rarely see the MINI trademarked emblem except in his pictures of the cars. When he mentions the MINI, he's referring to the car itself—there's no other way to talk about the car except to call it by its name. Burnside's blog has a well-chosen domain: dbmini.us. If you know that it's his blog and that it's about MINIs, the domain makes sense, but it's unlikely that someone would think that his blog is endorsed or owned by MINI. Since the domain contains the word *mini*, MINI could try to get his site removed by claiming the domain contains its trademark; however, given that MINI is well aware of Burnside's blog and podcast and has not raised any concerns, it is unlikely that the company will do so in the future.

You should also be aware of the possibility that someone could accuse you of trademark infringement if he wants to own your domain or if he wants you to stop using your domain. This was my theory when I heard about a situation involving Daniel Rothamel. He is a real estate agent and blogger in Virginia who was known as the Real Estate Zebra. In 2006, he registered the domain for his blog, realestatezebra.com. In 2011, he was sued by a real estate marketing company in Washington State that had a newsletter called *Zebra Report* and a blog called *Zebra Blog*.[140] The marketing company created the newsletter in 2005 and the blog in 2007. Neither side registered its marks with the USPTO, so each could claim common law trademark protection only where it was established. Given that all the publications were on the Internet, however, each

---

138. Don Burnside, *db's MINI adventures, news and pics*, last visited July 25, 2013, http://dbmini.us/.

139. *White Roof Radio*, last visited July 25, 2013, http://www.whiteroofradio.com/.

140. RERockstar, Lones Groups sues Daniel "Real Estate Zebra" Rothamel, Feb. 26, 2011, http://www.rerockstar.com/2011/technology/lones-group-sues-daniel-real-estate-zebra-rothamel/#axzz2VSmHLcn1.

side could try to make the argument that it was known nationwide; therefore, no one else could use a confusingly similar name.

It appeared the marketing company tried to use its newsletter to establish that it was using Real Estate Zebra first, and so it could exclude Rothamel from using the name on his blog. Rothamel could have made the argument that writing a blog is different from releasing a newsletter; therefore the marketing company was the senior user of *zebra* in regards to a newsletter but that did not establish the company as the first user of *zebra* for blogging. I think Rothamel had a valid argument that he used *zebra* in relation to real estate blogging first and that blogging for real estate is different than blogging for a marketing company. Additionally, Rothamel might have had a valid argument to make the marketing company stop using *zebra* in relation to its blog.

The marketing company sued Rothamel in federal court for $75,000 for trademark infringement and other offenses. The goals of the lawsuit may have been eliminating the competition by making Rothamel change his blog's name and domain and acquiring his domain for the company's use. If Rothamel's blog was more popular in the search results than its site, it may have sued him to make him stop using the name so the company could be the first result when someone searched for real estate zebra. The company's strategy may have been to scare him so he would offer to stop using the domain in exchange for it dropping the lawsuit.

If my theory is correct, the marketing company probably got what it wanted. Shortly after he was sued, Rothamel published a blog post stating that he would stop using the domain and his Twitter handle (@realestatezebra), and stop referring to himself as the Real Estate Zebra, in exchange for the company dropping the lawsuit.

If you have a blog and you don't register your name with the USPTO, you are at higher risk of being accused of trademark infringement. These cases are extremely fact specific, so there's no way to know in most cases if someone will have a valid claim against you for infringement based on your blog's name alone.

If you want to maximize your protection against trademark infringement claims, you should consult a trademark lawyer before you name your blog, do searches for your desired name on the USPTO and on the Internet, find a name that no one is using, and register your blog's name as a trademark. Until the blog's mark is accepted by the USPTO, you should put "TM" next to all the marks you want the exclusive right to use. If you ever get sued for trademark infringement or unfair competition, or if you receive a cease-and-desist letter because of your blog's name, consult a trademark lawyer immediately to assess whether the complaint against you is valid and/or worth fighting.

IN SUMMARY

- You may have trademark rights in your blog's name, domain, logo, and tagline. You will only have trademark rights under common law in your established geographic market if you do not register your mark with the USPTO.

- Since blogs often only exist online and may not sell any products, it may be quite difficult to determine your established market. You may be in a situation where a competitor will essentially steal your mark if he registers it first and you cannot prove where you've established your mark in commerce.

- You can obtain the exclusive rights to use your blog's name and other marks by registering them with the USPTO.

Chapter 12
JURISDICTIONAL ISSUES

Jurisdiction is, of course, the legal term that describes where you can be sued. Personal jurisdiction determines whether you can be sued in a particular state. Subject matter jurisdiction determines whether the case should be disputed in a state court or a federal court. There may be additional questions regarding which state's laws apply to your particular case.

If you are sued because of your blog, consider the court the plaintiff filed the suit in first. If you suspect the plaintiff filed the claim in the wrong state or the wrong court, file a motion to dismiss the case for lack of jurisdiction. The plaintiff could file suit against you again, but he would have to do it in a court that has personal jurisdiction over you and subject matter jurisdiction over the issue.

PERSONAL JURISDICTION

Personal jurisdiction describes where you can be sued geographically. You can be sued in the state where you live, where you conduct business, and where you were involved in an incident that led to you being sued. For instance, if you don't live or conduct business in

Arizona, but you rear end a car while you're traveling through Arizona on a road trip, you can expect to be sued in Arizona.

Once a blog post is released onto the Internet, it is accessible in all fifty states as long as there is an Internet connection. If you write about a person or company on your blog, and they claim that your blog caused them harm, the party will sue you in the state where the alleged damage occurred. You could be required to respond to the lawsuit filed against you in that state, even if you have never lived, traveled, or conducted any business there. Your blog may have created enough contact between you and the state where the subject of your post resides or does business that you could expect to be sued there.[141]

Following this logic, you can see that writing a blog puts you at potential risk of being sued in any state in the country, as long as the subject matter of your blog post resides or has a business presence there. A plaintiff can only sue you in the state where he has been injured. If you live and blog from California and you write about someone who lives and works in Texas, you can expect to be sued in Texas if he claims you harmed him. The Texan probably can't sue you in Alaska just to make it inconvenient for you to defend yourself there. He has to sue you where his injury occurred.

These cases are often fact-specific and will require a careful examination of the applicable laws. These cases are often based on state laws, which can vary from state to state. Always review the applicable state laws to determine whether writing a blog post is sufficient to establish jurisdiction.

SUBJECT MATTER JURISDICTION

Subject matter jurisdiction refers to whether a case can be heard in state or federal court. In general, if a case involves a state law, it is

---

141. International Shoe Co. v. Washington, 326 U.S. 310, 320-21 (1945). *See also* World-Wide Volk-swagen Corp. v. Woodson, 444 U.S. 286, 291-92 (1980).

heard in a state court. Likewise, cases based on federal law are disputed in federal court.

There are exceptions to this general rule. If a case involves both federal and state law violations, the laws that apply to the majority of the claims usually determine where the case will be decided.

The Copyright Act is a federal law. If you are sued for a copyright violation, you will be sued in federal court. Other lawsuits that can arise because of your blog (i.e., defamation, invasion of privacy, and intentional infliction of emotional distress) are based on state laws; therefore, you will likely be sued in a state court if you are sued for one of those offenses. There are state and federal trademark laws, so you can expect to be sued in a state or federal court for trademark infringement.

WHICH STATE LAW APPLIES?

Each state sets its own laws that are not otherwise covered by federal law, so when a lawsuit is based on a state law, what may be permissible behavior in your state may be illegal in another.

When you are sued because of your blog, the court will look to where the injury occurred. The court will most likely use the state law that applies in the state where the injury occurred. The good news is that these laws are generally similar from state to state; however, there are differences that can have a significant impact on the outcome of your case.

For example, Crystal Cox is a self-proclaimed "investigative blogger" in Montana. She writes a blog called Bankruptcy Corruption.[142] In one of her posts, she called Kevin Padrick, a lawyer in Oregon, "a thug, a thief, and a liar." Padrick sued Cox for defamation in Oregon,

---

142. *Crystal Cox Blogger ~ Investigative Blogger Crystal L. Cox,* last visited June 17, 2013, http://www.bankruptcycorruption.com.

the state where his reputation was damaged. Cox was required to travel to Oregon to defend herself using Oregon's laws.

Cox represented herself in the lawsuit and tried to use the Montana shield law to prevent the court from forcing her to reveal an information source. This law protects reporters from having to reveal the identity of confidential information sources. In Montana, her argument may have held water, but unfortunately for her, the lawsuit was governed by Oregon law, not Montana law. The Oregon shield law specifically states that you can't use the law as a defense in a civil defamation case.[143] Padrick won his case for defamation, and the court ordered Cox to pay him $2.5 million in damages.

When you say potentially disparaging things about a person or company on your blog, you open yourself up to being accused of wrongdoing. It's important that you know what you could be accused of and that you select your words carefully to avoid these problems. Even if you do nothing wrong, you could still be accused of violating a state or federal law. Ideally, you should be familiar with those laws before you publish the post so can position yourself to avoid lawsuits and effectively defend yourself if you are ever sued.

One way you can try to control the jurisdiction in the event there is a dispute related to your blog is with your website's terms of service. These terms are the contract you create with your users when they use your site. It is not a standard practice to have a terms of service for a website that is just a blog; however, you could put terms on your site which would manage your relationships with at least people who post comments on your work. Your terms of service could state that all disputes between you and a commenter must be resolved in your state and/or county and under your state's laws. You could also include provisions that require disputes to be resolved in mediation or arbitration if you'd like and that the commenter must reimburse your reasonable lawyers' fees if you prevail. If you

---

143. Oregon Shield Law, Or. Rev. Stat. §§ 44.510-44.540 (2013).

are going to control your relationships with your commenters with your terms of service, your website should include a notice that potential commenters should review the terms of service before commenting on your work since most bloggers do not appear to use terms of service in this way.

This strategy would likely only apply to disputes with people who leave comments on your blog. It would not likely apply to anyone you write about who does not leave comments on your website.

The Internet is accessible almost everywhere on the planet. It's possible you could be sued in another country because of your blog—one without the equivalent of the First Amendment or other American laws.[144] What is legal for you to write in the United States may be illegal in another country. It is unlikely that the average blogger who lives in the United States will be sued in a different country, but you may want to be mindful of where you travel and what you publish when traveling abroad.

IN SUMMARY

- Writing a blog post may create sufficient contact between you and the plaintiff's state to establish personal jurisdiction over you, even if you have never physically been in that state.

- If you are sued because of your blog, you will likely have to respond to the claim using the laws in the plaintiff's state, which may differ significantly from the laws in your home state. It's prudent to be aware of the differences between applicable state laws when writing critical or scathing posts about a person or entity.

---

144. Bodney, *supra* note 80.

Chapter 13

GETTING FIRED
BECAUSE OF YOUR BLOG

Yes, you can be fired because of your blog. If you're going to have a blog, you need to know the grounds on which you can and cannot be disciplined or fired because of what you say on the Internet.

Your employer is motivated to protect the company's reputation. The firm should have policies regarding acceptable conduct at work and policies regarding your behavior when you're on your own time. You should read your employment contract and employee handbook carefully to determine what limits your employer has placed on your blogging activities. There are likely policies against disclosing confidential company information and making negative statements about the company's clients. If you violate these rules on your blog, you can be fired (and possibly face bar sanctions).

If you are an at-will employee, you can be fired for any reason or for no reason. That means you could be fired because of your blog just because the partners don't like it, even if it has nothing to do with your job. You should be careful about blogging about anything related to your employment or any topic that the partners (or the board of directors, if you're in-house counsel) might find offensive if you are an at-will employee. Your employer can likely fire you for anything you post on your personal blog, not just blogs that are work related, as long as there isn't a law that prohibits your employer from firing you. If you are fired for an illegal reason, such as because of your race, religion, or disability, you have options for recourse.

If you are a legal blogger for your firm or company, it is unlikely that you'll post anything that will directly lead to your termination. When a company decides to start an official company blog, there should be a strategy meeting with the executive team, the marketing team, and the bloggers to create guidelines so that your posts are in alignment with the company's image and the goals of the blog. I suspect most firms will also create some type of review process where every post will be approved before it appears on the firm's website.

NATIONAL LABOR RELATIONS ACT

The National Labor Relations Act (NLRA) is a federal law that gives private-sector employees the ability to meet to discuss their wages and work conditions.[145] Employees may also discuss these topics with their employer without repercussion. This law went into effect in 1935 and it was designed to protect unions and union-like activities. The NLRA protects employees, not supervisors (and no, you can't get around this law by declaring that everyone in the company is a supervisor). This law also does not apply to people in public-sector jobs. The NLRA is enforced by the National Labor Relations Board (NLRB), a federal agency.

Your employer cannot have a policy that interferes with your rights under the NLRA. He can't restrict your ability to talk about wages or work conditions with your fellow employees. He also can't prohibit you from disclosing to others what company you work for, including on online forums. Some private-sector employers have

---

145. National Labor Relations Act, 29 U.S.C. §§ 151–169 (2012).

implemented policies that prohibit employees from disclosing their employer's name, which results in employees creating LinkedIn profiles where they describe their employer's purpose or what industry they work in without sharing the company's name.

The NLRA does not put any limits on where employees and employers are allowed to have discussions about wages or work conditions. They may occur in private, in public, or on an online forum like a Facebook page or a blog. To qualify for protection under this law, there must be a "protected concerted activity," a group activity that involves multiple employees. This law does not protect your right to merely gripe, complain, or whine about your employer.

For example, the NLRA protects your ability to make a post on a coworker's Facebook page about your dissatisfaction about your salary, billable hour requirements, or your work conditions. It doesn't have to be polite or respectful. You and your coworker could have a public conversation on your Facebook wall where you say something like, "It sucks that we're not getting a raise this year at Suem and Wynn Law Firm," and the firm likely can't fire you for that statement. If you had logged on to your own Facebook page where you were connected with none of your coworkers and posted, "I hate my bosses at Payne and Suffrin Law Firm" or even "My job sucks," you might get fired because you weren't communicating with your fellow employees or your employer and you weren't discussing wages or work conditions. You were just ranting.

Ranting about work to your coworkers may not be enough to qualify as a protected concerted activity. In 2013, the NLRB ruled that an employee was not illegally fired for posting on her Facebook page a taunt aimed at her employer that included the statement, "FIRE ME...MAKE my day."[146] The employer subsequently fired

---

146. Sara Hutchins Jodka, "When Employee Taunts Employer via Facebook to 'FIRE ME. ...Make my day. . .' NLRB Memo Concludes the Employer Can Go For It," *Employer Law Report*, May 22, 2013, http://www.employerlawreport.com/2013/05/articles/labor-relations/when-employee-taunts-employer-via-facebook-to-fire-me-make-my-day-nlrb-memo-concludes-the-employer-

this employee after learning about this statement. Despite the fact that this statement was made during an online conversation that included coworkers, the NLRB ruled that this was "griping," not a protected discussion about workplace concerns. Simply being in the physical or virtual presence of your coworkers does not automatically make your conversation a protected concerted activity.

If you are disciplined or fired when you believe you were engaged in a protected concerted activity, you can submit a complaint against your employer to the NLRB. The NLRB will investigate your claim and if it finds that your claim has merit, your employer could be ordered to pay you back wages and damages and possibly offer you your job back. The NLRB will encourage the parties to reach a settlement if possible, but if you and your possibly former employer cannot come to an agreement, the NLRB will resolve the situation.

WHAT YOU CAN BLOG ABOUT WITHOUT BEING FIRED

If you make statements on your blog about your work conditions and your coworkers leave comments with their thoughts, that exchange should be protected by the NLRA. The law should also protect you if post a summary of the conversation about wages or work conditions that you had with your coworkers.[147] As long as your post somehow involves your coworkers and pertains only to wages and/or work conditions, you should be protected by the NLRA.

Additionally, you will also be protected by the NLRA if you write a post about wages and work conditions that's written to inspire action or conversation among your coworkers. Even if no such conversation results from it, you will still be protected by the law

---

can-go-for-it/#ixzz2Xu8A6c3a.

147. Melanie Trottman, "What Workers Can—and Can't—Do on Facebook," *Wall Street Journal*, December 2, 2011, http://online.wsj.com/article/SB1000142405297020401200457707252111 0400592.html#ixzz1goylmksU.

because you were attempting to initiate a protected concerted activity. You will also be protected by the NLRA if you write a post on behalf of yourself and your fellow employees.

You should be able to do some name-calling on your blog if you're not threatening anyone and if it's part of a protected concerted activity. There was a situation where the NLRB ruled that an employee was wrongfully fired when she called her boss a "scumbag" on Facebook. She made the statement during a conversation with her fellow employees about their supervisors at work. The NLRB found that they were engaged in a protected concerted activity so she was permitted to call her boss a "scumbag" in this context without repercussion.[148] If the same discussion occurred on a blog post, it should also be protected.

If you are an outspoken blogger or want to write about your work experience, be aware of the line between what you *can* legally write and what you *should* write. When you are particularly harsh and attack people via your blog, you may be harming your reputation. It could hurt your chances for promotions within your company and it may make it more difficult for you to be hired by another firm if you wish to leave your current position. Another firm may be less likely to hire you after they see the way you spoke about your former employer while you were working there. Always consider the big picture before releasing a strongly worded post. You don't want today's righteous indignation to become tomorrow's regret.

This is an area of law that is constantly evolving, which is why I use the word *should* instead of *will*. You should check the most recent report from the NLRB for the most up-to-date information about what online behaviors are protected by the NLRA.

---

148. Melanie Trottman, "For Angry Employees, Legal Cover for Rants," *Wall Street Journal*, December 2, 2011, http://online.wsj.com/article/SB1000142405297020371070457704982280971033 2.html?KEYWORDS=facebook+fired.

HOW YOUR BLOG CAN GET YOU FIRED

The NLRA protects concerted activities, not your ability to write blog posts about how much you dislike your job, coworkers, or clients. You can be fired if you are complaining on behalf of only yourself without any "intended or actual group action to improve working conditions."[149] You may want to think twice if you're having a bad day and you're looking to blow off steam because you're annoyed with your clients, hate your opposing counsel, or think your judge is an idiot. Your blog may not be the best forum to vent your frustration.

The NLRA allows you to call someone a name or disrespect them if it occurs as part of a protected concerted activity; however, it does not protect you if you make any threats. If you make a statement that can be construed as a threat of violence against a person or the company, you could be fired. The NLRB will consider the context of your statement to determine whether you made a threat and if your employer had grounds for firing you for making the threat.

You may also want to be thoughtful about what you say in jest that might be interpreted as a serious threat. In 2013, a Texas teenager was arrested after he posted a statement on Facebook that he was "going to go shoot up a school full of kids and eat their still beating hearts."[150] Even though the statement was followed by "lol" (laugh out loud) and "jk" (joke), the teen was arrested for "making a 'terroristic threat.'"

You can also be fired if you make statements in your blog that violate your employment contract, such as disclosing company trade secrets or making disrespectful statements about the company that are not part of a protected, concerted activity. Furthermore you could face discipline from your employer, your state bar association,

---

149. Trottman, *supra* note 148.

150. Lorenzo Franceschi-Bicchierai, "Texas Teenager Arrested for Violent Facebook Comment," Mashable, June 29, 2013, http://mashable.com/2013/06/28/texas-teenager-arrested-facebook-comment/.

and/or the court if you use your blog to engage in conduct that violates the lawyer-client privilege or conduct that could be construed as an ex parte communication.

THIS IS A GRAY AREA

The rulings by the NLRB have given employees and employers some dos and don'ts regarding employee online behavior. However, there are still many unanswered questions, such as whether an employee who publishes a negative post about the employer from a workplace computer can be disciplined, and where the line between protected and unprotected name-calling falls.[151] The answers to these questions will likely depend of the details of the each situation, including the company's policies, the context of each statement, and your employment contract.

Having a blog makes you more vulnerable than employees who have other social media profiles because your blog is available for everyone to see. On Facebook and Twitter you can use privacy settings to somewhat limit who sees your posts, but on a blog, your words are shared with the entire Internet-accessible world. If you blog about your work, you are more likely to be targeted for disciplinary action than an employee who doesn't blog about work. If your employer has a clear social media policy that complies with the NLRA, it will be easier for you to know what your dos and don'ts are. If you employer doesn't have a social media policy, ask for one, and ask your employer to include examples of acceptable and unacceptable online behavior.

If you want to blog about your experiences as a lawyer from a practitioner or law practice management perspective, and include examples from your professional life, you may want to have a discussion with your employer in advance to determine what would be

---

151. Id.

appropriate for you to blog about, especially if you are blogging under your real name or the firm's name.

When in doubt, don't share information about your work on your blog or anywhere else online until you know that your communication qualifies as a protected concerted activity. You may want to consult a lawyer who is familiar with the NLRA to help you determine what you can and can't say on your blog under the law and your employment contract. If you are fired or disciplined because of your blog and you believe you were engaged in a protected concerted activity, file a complaint against your employer with the NLRB.

IN SUMMARY

- If you are an at-will employee, you can be fired simply because your company dislikes your personal blog, so long as the reason why they dislike it is not illegal or a violation of your employment contract.

- If you are disciplined or fired because of a work-related post on your blog and the post qualifies as a protected concerted activity, you may have recourse under the National Labor Relations Act. This may include conversations or posts on the Internet that are viewable by anyone that contain name-calling and other disrespectful language.

- Pure rants and threats are not protected by the National Labor Relations Act.

- You may face other negative consequences as a result of your blog—such as damage to your reputation and ability to advance within your firm.

Chapter 14

GETTING ARRESTED BECAUSE OF YOUR BLOG

While the First Amendment protects most of what you post online, not all speech is protected. In only a few cases has a person been accused of committing a crime with an online post, but if something is illegal to publish in a newspaper, putting it on your blog is also probably illegal.

It is unlikely that a lawyer or other legal professional would say something on his personal blog that would lead to his arrest. I suspect it would take an irate employee for a blogger to be arrested for a post on his firm's blog. However, it is possible that you could be arrested because of a blog post; therefore, you should be aware of the types of crimes you could be accused of committing via your blog.

THREATS OF VIOLENCE

In general, it's illegal to threaten someone with violence. Some state laws for assault require physical contact between the assailant and victim; however, other state assault laws assert that a person commits assault when his words make a reasonable person afraid of an imminent physical injury. If the assault law doesn't specify what methods must be used to create this apprehension, it's possible that someone will make a valid argument that a threat on a blog is sufficient to charge a blogger with assault.

In Britain, there has already been one such arrest when a woman posted a death threat on Facebook.[152] There was also a similar incident on Twitter; Paul Chambers became angry when the airport closed because of snow and disrupted his travel plans. He tweeted, "You've got a week and a bit to get your s**t together, otherwise I'm blowing the airport sky high!"[153] The authorities took his threats seriously and he was ultimately convicted of sending menacing messages over a public electronic communications network.

THREATS AGAINST THE PRESIDENT OF THE UNITED STATES

Whatever you do on your blog, don't do anything that might look like you're making a threat against the president of the United States. The Secret Service appears to be patrolling the Internet for posts that threaten the president's life, and they take every potential threat seriously, even when it originates from a seemingly innocent person. Julia Wilson was a fourteen year-old student who posted a picture of then-president George W. Bush on her MySpace page with the words *Kill Bush* across it.[154] The Secret Service showed up at her school and pulled her out of class for questioning. According

---

152. Luke Salkeld, "Facebook bully jailed: Death threat girl, 18, is first person put behind bars for vicious Internet campaign," *Daily Mail News*, Aug. 21, 2009, http://www.dailymail.co.uk/news/article-1208147/First-cyberbully-jailed-Facebook-death-threats.html#ixzz1x51tsbZX.

153. David Ma, "How Not To Use Social Media, *Techblawg*, May 27, 2010, http://techblawg.ca/2010/05/27/how-not-to-use-social-media/.

154. "Teen Questioned Over Online Threats Against President Bush," Associated Press, Oct. 14, 2006, http://www.foxnews.com/story/0,2933,220779,00.html#ixzz1x54a1E00. *See the photo at* Fred Soto, "Julia Wilson, "Did a teen threaten national security?," *Whitehouser*, Oct. 14, 2006, http://whitehouser.com/war/julia-wilson-national-security-threat/.

to the report, she didn't know that threatening the president was a federal offense.

The First Amendment gives you the ability to express your dissatisfaction with the administration, but it doesn't extend to potential death threats. If your blog has a political bent, such as a public policy blog, you need to be careful that when you are speaking harshly about the president that it will not be misinterpreted as a threat.

CYBERHARASSMENT

Most states have laws against using social media, text messages, and e-mail to bully or harass people. These laws also prohibit you from harassing people by creating websites about them. Law enforcement has begun taking these cases more seriously, especially since Megan Meier committed suicide in 2006. She took her own life after being told the world would be better without her via a message on MySpace.[155]

Megan was a thirteen year-old girl who struggled with attention deficit disorder, being overweight, and depression. Megan befriended a boy named Josh on MySpace who acted like her friend. On October 16, 2006, Josh unexpectedly sent her a message that said, "You are a bad person and everybody hates you. Have a shitty rest of your life. The world would be a better place without you." Megan hanged herself shortly after receiving that message and died the next day. Megan's parents later learned that Josh wasn't a real person but was a fake profile created by the parents of one of Megan's former friends with whom Megan had had a falling out. Although no criminal charges were filed against the parents who created the fake profile, law enforcement took the situation seriously and conducted a full investigation.

---

155. Megan Meier's Story, Megan Meier Foundation, last visited June 30, 2013, http://www.megan-meierfoundation.org/megansStory.php..

If there is someone you despise, you may want to write strongly worded posts about him. If you take it too far, you may be breaking the harassment law in your state or the state where your victim lives. If someone commits suicide because you bullied or harassed him on your blog, you could be held criminally liable.

ILLEGAL SALES

The Internet provides numerous forums to sell your possessions; however, it's illegal to sell certain items and services such as drugs, human body parts, stolen property, and sex. Selling these things is illegal, in person or online.

If you are accused of illegally selling something on Craigslist or eBay, you might have a chance to avoid punishment if you can prove that you didn't create the illegal online ad. It will be harder to make this argument if you are selling illegal goods or service from your personal website, especially if no one else is an administrator on your site or knows your password.

SOLICITATION

You can commit solicitation via your blog if you command, encourage, or request that your readers commit a particular crime. If your state criminal laws prohibit asking someone in person to commit a crime (regardless of the target's response), it is also likely illegal to solicit your readers via your blog to commit a crime. My research for this book did not reveal any instances where this has happened, but I would not be surprised to learn about a person being arrested for solicitation if he uses his blog to encourage others to commit a crime. You can be convicted of solicitation for asking your readers to commit a crime, even if no one does it.

Always remember that your blog can be used as evidence against you if you are arrested. There has been at least one case where a sex offender was given a harsher sentence when the judge held that the offender's blog indicated that he could not follow the court's orders or control his actions.[156] His designation was changed from being a "sex offender" to a "sexual predator" when he created a post aimed at his victim.

One of my rules of thumb for social media is only post information on the Internet that you would put on the front page of the newspaper. Following this rule will help you avoid being in a situation where your posts could be used against you, and you will be less likely to say something that will come back to haunt you.

IN SUMMARY

- When you write strongly worded posts, be careful not to cross the line and say something that could be interpreted as a threat or cyberharassment.

- If you encourage your readers to take action, make sure you don't inadvertently ask them to commit a crime.

---

156. State v. Sweeney, 2006 Ohio 4874, ¶14 (Ohio Court of Appeals, 5th Appellate Dist. 2006).

Chapter 15
DEATH BY BLOGGING

There have been too many situations where someone has been killed because of what he posted online, like the man who murdered his wife after he saw that she changed her marital status on Facebook to "single."[157] There will always be a risk that people will become so enraged after reading your blog that they want to harm you, though this is less likely to occur with a legal blog than a personal one. There are even some instances where your blog could get you killed.

In the United States, you have to be convicted of homicide; a crime that was committed in conjunction with a homicide, rape, criminal assault; or something equally heinous to be sentenced to death. It's pretty difficult, if not impossible, to commit one of these crimes via the words on your blog. There are other countries, however, where you can commit a crime that is punishable by death by expressing your views or beliefs.

---

157. Marshall Kirkpatrick, "Facebook Murder Reflects Cultural Shifts," *Read Write Web*, Jan. 22, 2009 http://www.readwriteweb.com/archives/facebook_murder_reflects_drama.php.

I did some research into other countries' laws and found a handful of crimes that are punishable by death that you could potentially commit with your blog.[158]

- Afghanistan: atheism; homosexuality
- Bahrain: defiance of military orders in time of war or martial law; plotting to topple the regime; threatening the life of the emir
- Botswana: mutiny
- Belarus: conspiracy to seize power
- China: corruption; endangering national security
- Egypt: treason
- Ethiopia: outrages against the constitution; treason
- Gambia: treason
- India: treason
- Iran: atheism; crimes against chastity; homosexuality
- Libya: attempting to forcibly change the form of government; high treason
- Mauritania: atheism
- North Korea: plots against national sovereignty—includes attempting to leave the country; treason
- Pakistan: atheism; blasphemy
- Saudi Arabia: atheism; sexual misconduct; witchcraft
- Singapore: treason
- South Sudan: treason
- Sudan: acts that may endanger the independence or unity of the state; atheism; waging war against the state

---

158. *Freedom of Thought 2012: A Global Report on Discrimination Against Humanists, Atheists and the Nonreligious*, International Humanist and Ethical Union, last visited July 8, 2013, http://iheu.org/files/IHEU%20Freedom%20of%20Thought%202012.pdf; "Use of Capital Punishment by Country," *Wikipedia*, last visited July 8, 2013, http://en.wikipedia.org/wiki/Use_of_capital_punishment_by_country. (Yes, I used *Wikipedia* as a source—verify this information if you have a case related to this issue.)

- Syria: membership in the Muslim Brotherhood; verbal opposition to the government
- The Maldives: atheism
- United Arab Emirates: treason
- Vietnam: undermining peace
- Yemen: adultery; homosexuality

When it comes to crimes committed via blogs, the first question that arises is jurisdiction. Since a blog can be accessed anywhere there's an Internet connection, a prosecutor would have to prove the court had jurisdiction over you. This would be hard to do if you put something in a blog post that was illegal in one country but you published the blog post while you were physically in a different country. Even if criminal charges were filed against you in that country, it's unlikely that they would go through the trouble of trying to expedite you, unless you had a direct connection to that country.

From this list, it is obviously highly unlikely that a legal blogger would use his blog to commit a crime that is punishable by death. A political blogger could conceivably commit such a crime, but even then, he would probably need to create a huge following that had direct implications in the country whose laws it was breaking before the government would be concerned with the blogger's writings. Most legal bloggers write about topics that are related to law practice management or common client issues, neither of which is likely to break the laws in any country.

An American citizen's best chance for death by blogging would be to go to another country and then post something that violated local laws. For example, if you travelled to Iran and posted a blog from your hotel room that said that you were gay, law enforcement in Iran might be able to arrest you for homosexuality. If you wrote the same post in the United States and never traveled to Iran, law enforcement there wouldn't be able to arrest you because they have no law enforcement authority for acts that occur outside Iran's borders.

Let's look at a more complicated example. What if a Syrian citizen was studying in the United States on a student visa, had a blog that was hosted in the United States, and published a blog post from the United States in which he declared his membership in the Muslim Brotherhood? Would Syria have jurisdiction to charge him with a crime and the authority to kill him if he ever returned to Syria? This is a gray area with many unanswered questions.

If you are a well-known blogger and you say something on your blog that would be a crime in another country, your safest course of action is to avoid traveling there. It's probably unlikely that a country would care what you put on your blog unless you have some influence in that country. However, you may want to be careful if you're famous—or infamous—in a country where your words might violate a local law.

IN SUMMARY

- It is possible that you could write a blog post that violates a law in a country—other than the United States—where the punishment could be death.

- It's highly unlikely, even if you break such a law, that the government in one of those countries would seek to arrest you, unless you were physically present in the country and causing enough problems that the government became aware of your website.

Chapter 16

BENEFITS OF BEING A LEGAL BLOGGER

Prior to the Internet, you needed a publisher if you wanted to reach a broad audience. Now anyone with an Internet connection can easily buy a domain and create a forum to reach their audience.

Earlier this year, I looked into my options for marketing my firm. Even when I was looking into traditional marketing strategies, advertising agencies were giving me online marketing campaign proposals. This appears to be the most effective and efficient way to reach a target audience.

As a business owner, I attend my fair share of networking events and professional development seminars. "Content is king" is a phrase I hear at every seminar on social media marketing, whether it's an event for lawyers in particular or all business professionals. The key to developing an online presence and a reputation for your firm and yourself individually is to create quality content aimed at providing value for your audience.

If you don't have a blog or you've created one but still aren't sure how it's supposed to help you, you might be wondering how having a blog is an asset. Let me count the ways....

ESTABLISH EXPERTISE AND BUILD CREDIBILITY

"Blogging remains the clearest and most definitive medium for demonstrating expertise on the web."[159] This is absolutely true. Having a blog is one of the best ways to build your credibility and carve out a niche for yourself within your area of practice.

The benefit of having a blog is it gives you the ability to demonstrate your knowledge instead of simply telling people what you do. For example, you can tell people that your practice focuses on DUI defense or you can demonstrate what you know by having a blog that addresses common client questions, provides explanations on changes to the DUI laws, and explains current events where driving under the influence was an issue. If your goal for having blog is to reach potential clients, you will have a useful platform for translating complicated legalese into plain English, providing explanations using layman's terms, and telling demonstrative stories using real-life examples

One of the easiest ways to establish a niche area of practice is to regularly blog about that topic. Flash mob law is one of my legal niches. I regularly write posts that analyze various flash mobs from a legal perspective.[160] Since I'm one of only a few lawyers who claim to practice flash mob law, my blog may be the only post written by a lawyer a person could find if he wanted to understand the legalities of public pillow fights, the annual global No Pants Subway Ride, or what level of authority mall cops really have if they confront you during your flash mob in their building.

Maintaining a blog is a much more effective way to show your expertise in an area of law compared to a static website. Most

---

159. Kevin O'Keefe, "Looking to Demonstrate Expertise as Lawyer? Blog," *Real Lawyers Have Blogs*, December 22, 2012, http://kevin.lexblog.com/2012/12/22/looking-to-demonstrate-expertise-as-lawyer-blog/.

160. Flash Mob Law, Carter Law Firm, last visited August 6, 2013, http://carterlawaz.com/practice-areas/flash-mob-law/.

websites are static; law firm websites are very static. They contain general information about the firm's philosophy, its practice areas, and biographies of its lawyers. Conversely, blogs are more timely. Blog posts can more easily react to current events and hot topics. The standard blog format is reverse chronological order, so a person researching you or your firm can see that you place value on keeping up with developments in your area of practice and how they affect clients as long as you update your blog regularly.

Gary Vaynerchuk is a leading expert on social media marketing. He constantly advises people that the purpose of having a blog is to provide value. Your blog should always be viewed and treated as useful resource and information hub for your readers.[161] Providing high quality and useful content will give clients and prospective clients a sense of security and trust that you will be able to understand and help them because your writings have already demonstrated that you understand their specific concerns.

LEVERAGE YOUR BLOG FOR OTHER OPPORTUNITIES

Having a blog can help you establish yourself as the go-to authority in your area of law.[162] You can leverage this reputation to obtain speaking engagements and create opportunities to be used as a media source. You are more likely to be viewed as a credible source if you have written blog posts on the subject that a reporter needs information about for an upcoming article or TV news story.

I leverage my blog posts to demonstrate my knowledge in areas of law frequently when I respond to opportunities on Help A Reporter

---

161. Ruth Carter, Gary Vaynerchuk: "Find Your Social Media 'Right Hook,'" *Attorney at Work*, February 12, 2013, http://www.attorneyatwork.com/gary-vaynerchuk-find-your-social-media-right-hook/.

162. "Technology Costs Spinning Out of Control? Tech Experts' Tips for Cutting Back (and What No Lawyer Should Do Without)," *Law Practice Magazine*, April/May 2006, http://www.american-bar.org/publications/law_practice_home/law_practice_archive/lpm_magazine_articles_v32_is3_an2.html.

Out (HARO).[163] HARO is a publicity service reporters use to find sources. HARO compiles the queries and sends an e-mail containing these opportunities to its thousands of subscribers three times a day each weekday. Each e-mail contains dozens of opportunities to be used as a source. I typically respond to one or two queries a week where I would like to be used as a source of legal expertise. Whenever possible, I include links to pertinent blog posts I've written on the subject to show the reporter that I would be a useful source for the article. I suspect my blog posts increase the likelihood of being chosen over a potential source who has not written blog posts on the subject matter. Leveraging my blog in responses to HARO postings has led to at least a dozen interviews for various news outlets.

In addition to responding to HARO queries, I also send local reporters links to my blog posts related to current events, and I let them know that I'm available if they wish to interview me. I'm most likely to do this when a current events story has a legal angle, and laymen might benefit from hearing a lawyer explain the related legalities. For example, a blog post I wrote about copyright infringement on Pinterest led to an invitation to be part of a news segment about the topic, including the risk Pinterest users take when they are not mindful about what they are pinning and the damages they could be ordered to pay if they are sued for infringement. The blog post on the topic is my way of making an introduction and showing my expertise on the subject matter.

Furthermore, blogging appears to be good for business. The *ABA Journal* recently shared an interview in which Kevin O'Keefe reported that seventy-eight percent of the highest grossing law firms in the United States had blogs and that there was a correlation between blogging and increased revenue.[164]

---

163. Help A Reporter Out, last visited August 6, 2013, http://www.helpareporter.com/.

164. Lee Rawles, "Firms with blogs have seen increased revenue; is there a correlation?" (video), *ABA Journal*, Jun. 6, 2013, http://www.abajournal.com/news/article/bvideo_lexblog_founder_firms_with_blogs_have_seen_increased_revenue/?utm_source=maestro&utm_medium=

SHOW YOUR PERSONALITY

A blog is an effective way to share your personality as well as your knowledge with your audience. Your readers will get a glimpse into who you are based on the topics you write about, your word selection, your writing style, and the images you use in your posts. If your blog is separate from the law firm's site, you can have a separate biography that is geared towards what your readers want to know about you beyond where you went to law school and your practice areas.

Even though your blog will primarily have a legal focus, not every post has to be focused on legal topics. You may wish to consider writing on other topics sporadically that are pertinent to you as a person but that are separate from your legal career. You might write posts about an issue that's important to you or your family, or posts about your hobbies. These posts show that you are a real person who is authentic in your writings.

Jay Thompson was a realtor and now works as the Director for Industry Outreach and Social Media for Zillow. He is a well-regarded real estate blogger who maintains a website called The Phoenix Real Estate Guy.[165] Most of his posts focus on topics related to real estate, but he occasionally writes about issues from his personal life—like his experience having and recovering from a heart attack—and he also invites his friends in the real estate world to write posts about their personal lives. Real estate is not a pertinent issue in my everyday life, but because I've gotten to know and love Jay through his blog and in real life, he is my go-to guy for all my real estate needs.

Lawyers can integrate their personalities into their blog posts too. It can be part of a legal post, like when I included information

---

email&utm_campaign=weekly_email.
165. *The Phoenix Real Estate Guy*, last visited August 6, 2013, http://www.phoenixrealestateguy.com/.

and a picture of my dog Rosie in a post about solo lawyers and lone-liness.[166] Likewise, you can write posts that have nothing to do about the practice of law. My favorite military criminal defense lawyer is Eric Mayer. His blog is the Unwashed Advocate, and he writes posts about current legal events in the military and about whatever seems to strike his fancy, such as his love of Leo's maple bacon donuts.[167] I love his delightfully blunt and sarcastic nature. I know Eric in real life, and I love that his writing style is exactly like the way he speaks.

One thing I've learned about the practice of law is that people hire people, not law firms. Your firm's reputation may get you an initial meeting with a potential client, but he is less likely to hire the firm if he doesn't like the lawyer assigned to him. When you let your personality shine through in your blog posts, you will build your reputation with your readers based on the content of your posts, and they will like you before you've ever said one word directly to them when they come to you as a prospective client. Being authentic in your writings creates the foundation for your future in-person relationships with your audience.

When it comes to your blog, be real and personable. It's about making connections with others, not pontificating from your digital platform. When you start your blog, be sure to decide in advance what topics are off limits. Some people choose never to mention their children on their blogs. Others give their children nicknames. To protect her granddaughter's privacy and safety, one of my blogger friends refers to her granddaughter as Small Child instead of using her real name in posts. There's no single right or wrong way to share your personality in your posts as long you are authentic.

---

166. Ruth Carter, "The Lonely Side of Solo Practice," *Attorney at Work*, March 5, 2013,
      http://www.attorneyatwork.com/the-lonely-side-of-solo-practice.
167. Eric Mayer, "Leo's Donuts: Setting the Bar at ∞", *Unwashed Advocate*, May 6, 2013,
      http://unwashedadvocate.com/2013/05/06/leos-donuts-setting-the-bar-at-∞.

BUILD RELATIONSHIPS THROUGH CONVERSATIONS

"Your blog is worthless if it doesn't engage your reader."[168] Each post you write should be the opening of a conversation with your readers. Even when the goal of your post is to share information or educate your audience, there can always be a dialogue in the comments section of the post.

Writing blog posts makes it easy for you to communicate with a large number of people and create mutually beneficial relationships with your readers.[169] There is a richness in the conversation and connections that can follow a post. Writing provides a wonderful opportunity to connect with potential clients and other professionals whom you otherwise would not have had an opportunity to meet. It's a wonderful way to build your local and global network.

When you are creating your blog, determine who your target audience is and speak to their needs and in their language. This will make you appear accessible. You want to talk *with* your audience not *at* them. One tip I've heard from multiple sources is the power of storytelling. Gary Vaynerchuk said you "can't underestimate the benefit of telling your story. We remember stories more than we remember facts. Telling your story will help drive your desired results."[170] You can tell your story, your clients' stories (within the limits set by your state bar's ethical rules), and the stories of others who fit into your profile of your ideal clients. People connect with your stories and by doing so, they will connect with you.

---

168. Donna Seyle, "Law Bloggers: Are Your Readers Bored Yet?", *Attorney at Work*, August 11, 2011, http://www.attorneyatwork.com/law-bloggers-are-your-readers-bored-yet/.
169. "Technology Costs Spinning Out of Control? Tech Experts' Tips for Cutting Back (and What No Lawyer Should Do Without)", *supra* note 163.
170. Carter, *supra* note 162.

BLOGGING IS A COMMITMENT

Creating a blog is not an event. It's a commitment to regularly add content and maintain your website. Too often, people start a blog with gusto and then after a few weeks they realize how much work it is, they get "too busy" to write new posts, and the next thing they know it's been six months since they've posted anything new. Even though there are over three thousand legal blogs listed on the *ABA Journal's* website, Kevin O'Keefe suspects that only ten to twenty percent of them are being used effectively.[171]

I'm not going to sugar-coat this—blogging takes time. Sometimes it takes a lot of time to select your topic, write the post, find an image to go with your post (yes, every blog post needs an image), put the post on your site, and take care of the post's tags for SEO purposes. For those of you who don't know, SEO stands for *search engine optimization*, and it helps your posts and your website show up higher in Internet search results.

I am a firm believer that bloggers should write on a schedule. My friend, Jeff Moriarty, helped me set up my personal blog, The Undeniable Ruth, in 2010. He told me that he would not help me unless I made the commitment to write at least one post a week for the first two years of having the site. I have not gone a week without releasing a new post since my site's inception. When you write and release material on a set schedule, your readers come to expect and look forward to it, just like someone might look forward to reading his favorite weekly newspaper column.

I release new posts on The Undeniable Ruth at 5:00 a.m. Arizona time every Tuesday and on Carter Law Firm's blog at 5:00 a.m. Arizona time every Thursday. That means that I'm not allowed to go to bed on Monday or Wednesday until my post for the next day

---

171. O'Keefe, *supra* note 160. See also *ABA Journal Blawg Directory*, last visited August 6, 2013, http://www.abajournal.com/blawgs/.

is written and loaded onto my site. I also try to maintain an editorial calendar, which helps provide pertinent topics to write about. This calendar is flexible, so it allows me to replace ideas for posts with hot topics and current events when I think they will benefit my readers. Sometimes I'll ask my connections on social media what they want me to write about too, which helps me understand what topics are important to them.

Writing blog posts is not enough though; you have to create *quality* content. If your writing and content is crap, your readers will move on to to bloggers who create useful and entertaining posts. According to legal blogger Jim Calloway, if your posts are poorly written or you don't post frequently enough, you blog can hurt your reputation instead of enhance it.[172] If you don't write frequently enough, anyone who comes to your site will see that you don't update it regularly and may assume that you're not keeping up with current events and developments in the law. If your work is poorly written, you'll never create a following.

Another benefit of regularly blogging is that you'll be adding fresh content to your blog or firm's blog on a regular basis. This is good for your SEO.

THE RISK OF GIVING IT AWAY FOR FREE

One of my concerns about maintaining a blog for my law firm was the possibility that people will read the blog instead of hiring me for personalized legal information. I've learned that this really shouldn't be a concern. There will always be people who want free information. These are the same people who e-mail or call you with "a quick question." They have no intention of hiring you; however, creating a relationship with them through your blog could turn them into a

---

172. "Technology Costs Spinning Out of Control? Tech Experts' Tips for Cutting Back (and What No Lawyer Should Do Without)," *supra* note 163.

referral source for you. Just make sure that you're acting within the limits of the rules of professional conduct by providing only general information and not giving the impression that you're giving legal advice through your blog.

I've learned that you never have to worry about "giving it away for free" on your blog. The clients who want to hire you will be happy to pay you to tell them the same information that's on your blog because they want to hear from you that the information you put in a general post applies to them and their situation. Your blog is a good place to show how complicated an issue is and why it is easier for a client with a legal question to hire a lawyer—he will not be able to determine his rights or the proper course of action by himself. These posts will provide clients with a sense of security that you are qualified to help them with their problems.

The practice of law is fact dependent, and the law needs to be applied to each client's situation. Presenting general information and telling stories of others' experiences on your site may pique a prospective client's interest in learning about how their situation compares. The only time you should be concerned about saying too much is when someone asks for advice in the comments on your blog. That's when you suggest that a consultation is the better forum to discuss all the intricacies of their situation.

Never forget that blogging is a communication tool, and it's not for everyone. Ernie Svenson says, "A lawyer should blog if he or she likes to write and craves the opportunity to discuss legal matters in the most public forum."[173] He also suggests that a law firm's blog can be a natural extension of your existing marking plan. If you have the commitment necessary to maintain a blog, you can use your blog as an integral component of your networking strategy.

---

173. *Id.*

IN SUMMARY

- Maintaining a blog can help you establish yourself as a credible professional in your area of law.

- Clients hire people, not law firms, so don't be afraid to show your personality through your writings.

- Always look for opportunities to use your blog to have conversations and build relationships with your audience.

- Create a writing schedule for your blog and stick to it.

Chapter 17

ETHICAL ISSUES WITH HAVING A LEGAL BLOG

A blog is an effective way for a lawyer or law firm to distinguish itself from its counterparts and/or inform current and potential clients about pertinent legal issues. Social media professionals will advise you that you have to create quality content for your readers, and your state bar's ethics counsel will remind you to execute your blog within the limits set by your state's rules of professional conduct.

There is an abundance of information you as a lawyer can share on a blog without overstepping the ethical limits of your license. In general, it is good practice to share information in the context that you are a lawyer in a particular practice area because it will "authenticate [you] as a reliable and trusted authority that is worth reading and citing."[174] However, you always need to be mindful of your state's ethical rules regarding advertising and solicitation.

---

174. Kevin O'Keefe, "New Florida legal ethics rules have little effect on law blogs," *Real Lawyers Have Blogs*, December 27, 2009, http://kevin.lexblog.com/2009/12/27/new-florida-legal-ethics-rules-have-little-effect-on-law-blogs/.

DOES A LEGAL BLOG CONSTITUTE ADVERTISING?

Rules 7.1–7.4 of the American Bar Association Model Rules of Professional Conduct apply to lawyer advertising and solicitation.[175] According to the model rules, lawyers are permitted to advertise their services in print and electronic media so long as they do not make any false or misleading statements. Please review your state's rules regarding advertising, which may include additional requirements, such as a prohibition of using testimonials, laudatory statements, and references to past cases.[176]

Many legal bloggers were concerned when a lawyer in Virginia was reprimanded and accused of advertising his services via his blog in *Hunter v. Virginia State Bar*. Some of the questions in the case were whether this blog was protected by the First Amendment and whether the blog constituted "commercial speech." Commercial speech is speech that "beckons business" or "proposes a commercial transaction."[177] The Virginia court held that Hunter's blog was protected by the First Amendment; however it decided this lawyer's blog constituted commercial speech because of the following four factors:

1. The lawyer's motivation for the blog was partially economic.

2. Most of the posts were about the lawyer's cases with favorable results, and "thus advertised his lawyering skills."

3. The blog was part of the law firm's website.

4. The "blog was non-interactive and did not allow for public discourse."[178]

---

175. Model Rules of Professional Conduct, American Bar Association, last visited July 11, 2013, http://www.americanbar.org/groups/professional_responsibility/publications/model_rules_of_professional_conduct/model_rules_of_professional_conduct_table_of_contents.html.

176. O'Keefe, *supra* note 175.

177. Comments for the Commission on Ethics 20/20, American Bar Association Standing Committee on the Delivery of Legal Services, January 19, 2012, http://www.americanbar.org/content/dam/aba/administrative/delivery_legal_services/ls_del_ethics_2020_memo.authcheckdam.pdf.

178. Renee Choy Ohlendorf, Attorney Blogger Runs Afoul of Ethics Rules on Advertising," *Liti-*

The court ruled that the lawyer needed to add an "advertising disclaimer" to his blog to be compliance with the Virginia State Bar ethical rules because his blog constituted commercial speech. This ruling suggests that all Virginia law firm websites might need this advertising disclaimer.

Initially, some legal bloggers were worried that their blogs would be classified as commercial speech as a result of this ruling. However, the blog in this case differs in several ways from other legal blogs. Most legal blog posts do not discuss the writer's or the firm's recent cases (though posts may be inspired by cases), but rather they contain resources, general legal information, and provide explanations of legal implications of current events or changes in law. These blog posts may not qualify as demonstrating the blogger's "lawyering skills."

This case could be used to challenge whether other legal blogs are commercial speech because there is likely an economic motivation for writing the blog—whether to market the firm or to make money directly from the blog by selling advertising or e-books. Additionally, many law firms have a blog as part of their law firm's website.

The *Hunter* case suggests that blogs should be treated as commercial speech because there is an economic motivation. The tempering argument is that blogs are no different from other networking events where people discuss who they are, what they do, and offer general information in response to common questions related to their practice area. A blog should be treated with the same level of scrutiny as in-person discussion with others if the subject matters are similar.

The Virginia court ruling suggests that one way a lawyer can differentiate his blog from the *Hunter* case is to allow comments. Making the blog interactive may make it appear to be more like a communication forum and less like advertising. Furthermore, allowing comments on your blog is good practice because your blog should be a forum to interact and create relationships with your readers. When you don't allow comments it suggests that you are talking at readers instead of providing an opportunity for them to speak with you.

Despite the *Hunter* case, there seems to be few problems with lawyers violating their state bars' ethical rules regarding advertising.[179] Alice Neece Mine, assistant director of the North Carolina State Bar, reported that most bar complaints related to lawyer advertising concerned direct mailings that did not have the proper disclaimers. Likewise, James McCauley, ethics counsel for the Virginia State Bar, reported that the majority of advertising complaints came from lawyers' competition, not their potential clients.

AVOIDING SOLICITATION

The Model Rules for Professional Conduct define *solicitation* as "a targeted communication initiated by the lawyer that is directed to a specific person and that offers to provide, or can reasonably be understood as offering to provide, legal services."[180] Additionally, communications made to the general public do not constitute solicitation, including communications made through a website.[181]

Lawyers whose state bar adopts this definition of *solicitation* will likely not be soliciting client through their blogs unless a post is directed at a particular person (which would be unprofessional). Of

---

179. Kevin O'Keefe, "Bar leaders: Lawyer's online marketing not drawing ethics' complaints," *Real Lawyers Have Blogs*, June 14, 2013, http://kevin.lexblog.com/2013/06/14/lawyers-online-marketing-not-drawing-ethics-complaints/.

180. Rule 7.3., Comment 1, Model Rules of Professional Conduct, American Bar Association, last visited July 11, 2013, http://www.americanbar.org/groups/professional_responsibility/publications/model_rules_of_professional_conduct/rule_7_3_direct_contact_with_prospective_clients/comment_on_rule_7_3.html.

181. Id.

course, legal bloggers should refer to their state bar's rules regarding solicitation. If a state defines solicitation as communications that "beckon business," a blogger bound by that rule may have to be more thoughtful and tactful about what he writes in each post. If he is pushing a transaction or service more than providing information, it could be solicitation.

When a state adopts the model rule's definition of *solicitation*, a blogger should not be worried about being accused of soliciting business via his blog by ending a post with a statement like, "Contact us for more information." This is an acceptable way to provide information to readers and end the communication by reminding them that the law firm has services for sale related to the topic if a reader is so inclined. It makes the law firm or lawyer more accessible to people who want to continue the conversation outside the forum provided by the blog.

DISCLAIMERS

Every legal blog needs a disclaimer. It should be a permanent fixture in the footer or sidebar of your website. You should refer to your state's ethical rules to determine if you need an "advertising disclaimer," like the one Hunter was required to add to his website. If advertising disclaimers are required on the legal blogs for lawyers in your state, they are likely required on every law firm's website in your state.

If your state does not require an advertising disclaimer on your website, a standard disclaimer should be sufficient. It should state that your blog provides general legal information and that it is not a substitute for personalized legal advice. Readers who need such advice should contact a lawyer for assistance. If you choose to discuss your cases on your blog, your disclaimer should include a statement that information regarding past cases does not provide a guarantee regarding any reader's situation. Here is the disclaimer that is currently on my law firm's blog:

> This website should only be used for informational purposes. It does not constitute legal advice, and it does not create an attorney-client relationship with anyone. If you need legal advice, please consult an attorney in your community.[182]

My disclaimer is pretty cut-and-dry, but you can make it more entertaining. My favorite disclaimer on a legal blog is on Eric Mayer's Unwashed Advocate:

> Do you have legal problems? Reading this blog will not help. In fact, it will probably make them worse, and it will definitely make you feel worse. You don't want that. If you think you may need legal representation, find yourself a good lawyer— preferably one who is recommended by other lawyers.
>
> INFORMATION ON THIS SITE IS NOT LEGAL ADVICE.
> The opinions expressed in this site represent only the opinions of the author(s) and are in no way intended as legal advice upon which you should rely. Every person's situation is different and requires an attorney to review the situation personally with you. They are opinions, and mine only.
>
> NO ATTORNEY-CLIENT RELATIONSHIP CREATED.
> This site does not create an attorney-client relationship. Such a relationship can only be accomplished by execution of an agreement between any author or contributor to this site and a prospective client.[183]

Other websites may not have a disclaimer in the sidebar or footer of the blog, but instead create a separate page on the site just for the disclaimer, with a link to it that is available on every page on the website. This extensive disclaimer is on the website for Snell and

---

182. Disclaimer, Carter Law Firm, last visited July 11, 2013, http://carterlawaz.com/blog/.

183. Warning and Legal Stuff, *Unwashed Advocate*, last visited July 11, 2013, http://unwashedadvocate.com/.

Wilmer, which is the biggest law firm in the Phoenix area and has nine offices in the western United States and Mexico:

> The information provided on the Snell & Wilmer web site is offered purely for informational purposes. It is not intended to create or promote an attorney-client relationship and does not constitute and should not be relied upon as legal advice. It is not intended to seek professional employment in any state where lawyers in the firm are not admitted to practice, or in any state where this web site would not comply with applicable requirements concerning advertisements and solicitations.
>
> We intend to make every attempt to keep this information current. We do not promise or guarantee, however, that the information is correct, complete or up-to-date, and Internet subscribers and online readers should not act based upon this information without seeking professional counsel from an attorney admitted to practice in your location.
>
> Transmission of information from the Snell & Wilmer web site is not intended to create, and its receipt does not constitute, an attorney-client relationship with Snell & Wilmer or any of its individual attorneys or personnel. If you elect to communicate with the firm, or any of its attorneys, through this web site, do not transmit any information about any matter (and particularly not any confidential information) that may involve you until the firm has agreed to represent you, and you have received confirmation of that fact in the form of a written engagement letter.[184]

You can decide how brief or extensive you want your disclaimer to be. Remember to be mindful of your audience. If your audience is non-lawyers who might be potential clients, they may not want to read an extensive disclaimer so it's best to keep it brief and written in layman's terms.

---

184. Legal Disclaimer, Snell & Wilmer L.L.P., last visited July 11, 2013, http://www.swlaw.com/legal/disclaimer.

BLOGGING ABOUT YOUR CASES

Whether you *can* blog about your cases and whether you *should* blog about your cases are two different questions. In general, anyone can blog about public information. This means that you may blog about your cases in regards to information that was disclosed in public court or information that is part of a public record, even if you were one of the lawyers who argued the case.[185] You should be wary of the *Hunter* decision so that you decrease the likelihood that your blog will be seen as advertising instead of information.

If you want to blog about your clients, review your state bar's ethical rules regarding advertising and disclosing information to ensure that you are in compliance. Additionally, you should check your law firm's rules regarding cases and make sure that the owners of the firm approve of the firm or its lawyers blogging about its cases, even when you remove the identifiable information about your clients.

When you want to blog about your clients, you should extend them the courtesy of at least informing them in advance that you will be blogging about the public information in their case. If your firm approves of this practice, clients should be informed at the beginning of the representation that information about them may appear on the firm's blog. You don't want your clients to feel blindsided by their lawyers.

If you wish to share information learned in confidence from a client, you would, of course, need the client's consent to do so. I don't encourage this. If a client wants to talk about his case once it is finished, that is his prerogative. It will reflect badly on the lawyer to disclose client information—even with permission—because it may give the impression that the lawyer pressured his client into

---

185. Kevin O'Keefe, "Virginia Court: First Amendment protection for lawyer-bloggers," *Real Lawyers Have Blogs*, June 15, 2012, http://kevin.lexblog.com/2012/06/15/virginia-court-first-amendment-protection-for-lawyer-bloggers/.

consenting. Additionally, a lawyer should be exceptionally thoughtful about discussing his cases on his blog. You do not want to insinuate that you disclose information in open court simply so it is on the public record and thus fair game for writing about on your blog. I often say, "Life is blog material," but this does not apply to client confidential information.

Furthermore, if you blog about your cases, it is best to wait until the case is fully resolved before blogging about it. You do not want to improperly influence the court, jury, or potential jurors with your blog. Moreover, blogging about your case while it is in progress may take your attention away from properly arguing the case on it merits, especially if you are one to aggrandize the details of the story.

RESPONDING TO REQUESTS FOR ADVICE

Despite your disclaimer that your blog only provides information, you will get comments on your blog posts or e-mails from your readers that include requests for legal advice. It's good practice to respond to these comments to show that you are aware of your comments and care about interacting with your readers; however, you shouldn't say anything that could be interpreted as providing the advice requested or that would give the impression that you are creating a lawyer-client relationship with the commenter. Instead, it's best to respond that the commenter should contact you or another lawyer to discuss the matter in a forum where the matter can be explored thoroughly and confidentially. This will protect you from an accusation that you're providing advice and show that you are thoughtful about their needs.

Conversely, if a commenter asks a general question that you've already blogged about, you can provide a link to that post with the caveat that the person should seek legal counsel for advice on their particular situation.

When choosing a topic to blog about, a good rule of thumb is to blog about topics that you would talk about in a public networking event. This will help you ensure that your topics are relevant to your readers and not crossing the line into providing legal advice. You can likely discuss who you are, provide general information about your work, and address common questions in a general sense.

When it comes to legal blogging and using social media as a lawyer, it is important to remember that these are communication forums, much like the town square or coffee shop. The ultimate purposes are to create relationships and exchange information with others and to build a word-of-mouth reputation.[186]

DISCLOSING RELATIONSHIPS WHEN YOU GET FREE MERCHANDISE AND OPPORTUNITIES

When you have a successful blog, you will be regarded as having influence over your readers. You can leverage this to get free products by offering to publish a review on your site, companies may send you free products with the hope that you'll write about them on your blog. Lawyers with legal blogs may be offered or could make offers to companies to get free books, gadgets, office supplies, and software related to their area of practice or running an effective practice. If you get free products or services and write about them on your blog, you must disclose your relationship with the company, regardless of whether you solicited the company to provide you with the items.

The Federal Trade Commission created a rule that went into effect in 2009 about endorsements and testimonials.[187] If you review products or give endorsements on your blog, you are required to be

---

186. Kevin O'Keefe, *supra* note 180.
187. Federal Trade Commission, "Guides Concerning Use of Endorsements and Testimonials in Advertising," 16 CFR §§ 255.0–255.5 (2013).

truthful and clear about your opinion. You must also disclose any relationships you have with any related company or person. This law requires you to divulge when you are compensated for providing an endorsement or testimonial for a product. This rule is particularly relevant to people who receive free products in exchange for reviews on their website or who receive free products from companies who hope that they'll write about it on their sites.

This law helps maintain a level of truthfulness and transparency when it comes to endorsements and product reviews. Before this rule went into effect, a company could give away free products or otherwise compensate people for giving positive reviews of their product and/or writing negative reviews about their competition's products with few consequences so long as the reviewer did not defame the company. The company could also direct its employees to manipulate review sites with fake positive and negative reviews of products and services. Before this rule, it was harder for consumers to have any faith in testimonials about products because it was difficult to differentiate the fake posts from the ones where a consumer provided an unbiased opinion. Since this rule was put in place, people are still writing fake reviews of companies and products; however, this law provides another option for recourse when it occurs.

This law applies equally to bloggers who write blogs about products as to people who leave comments about products on other people's blogs or other websites.[188] You must disclose your connection with advertisers and sellers when you have been paid to give your opinion about a product or received the product for free.[189] Complying with this rule can be as easy as adding a sentence to your post like, "Apple sent me this free iPad to use for a month, and here's

188. Evo Terra, "New FTC guidelines for bloggers are a bigger challenge for marketers," *A Simpler Way*, December 7, 2009, http://asimplerway.com/new-ftc-guidelines-for-bloggers-are-a-bigger-challenge-for-marketers/.

189. Federal Trade Commission," FTC Publishes Final Guides Governing Endorsements, Testimonials," October 5, 2009, http://www.ftc.gov/opa/2009/10/endortest.shtm.

what I think." The opinion you give about the free product or service must reflect your honest opinion about it. This law prohibits you from writing a positive review about a product simply because you got it for free.

LEGAL ISSUES RELATED TO TESTIMONIALS FROM CLIENTS AND PEER RECOMMENDATIONS

The reviews, testimonials, and recommendations for you from clients are also are subject to this rule. It is perfectly fine to inform clients where they may provide a recommendation for you (LinkedIn, Avvo, Yelp, etc.), but you want to be careful that you do not give the appearance that you pressure clients to provide favorable reviews for services. Additionally, it is likely a violation of your state bar's ethical rules to compensate clients for writing positive reviews about you as well as a violation of federal law.

This law also applies to peer-to-peer recommendations and endorsements of lawyers on websites like LinkedIn and Avvo. If you are going to write a recommendation for a colleague on one of these sites, you can only tell the truth about the person based on your experience.

PAID LINKS

Once you have a blog, you may be contacted by people who want to you to put a link to their website in one of your existing posts. They may offer to pay you or ask to exchange links, meaning they will link to your site if you agree to add a link to their website on yours. The person may even ask you to alter your previously-released work to better accommodate a link to their website. Providing a link to a site may look like an endorsement if you're not linking to a site strictly for informational purposes. If you are being compensated for providing a link, that may be an activity that falls under the umbrella of the FTC regulation regarding endorsements.

When I started receiving these offers, I informed the person that if I accepted their offer I must disclose that I was being compensated for adding the link to a post. Many people disliked hearing this because they don't want people to know that it's a paid link and that I didn't support the website solely on my own volition based on what I thought would be valuable for my readers. They wanted readers to think that I truly endorsed their idea or product. Failing to disclose this relationship would go against the spirit of transparency that underlies this regulation. These people lose interest in having me add a link to their website when I inform them that I would have to disclose my relationship with them.

COMPLIANCE AND PENALTIES FOR VIOLATING THIS RULE

Unfortunately, this rule is also quite easy to break. If you forget to disclose your relationship when giving an endorsement, you can be fined up to $11,000 per violation. You are more likely to be fined a higher amount if you are deceptive in your published opinions about products and services.[190] You must conspicuously disclose on your blogs when you are being compensated for your opinions.[191] You can also be liable for any misleading or unsubstantiated statements you make in your testimonial.[192]

This fine can be charged to the blogger who made the false or the biased statement or the company that solicited the blogger to provide the review. In determining who should be charged, I suspect the FTC examines the relationship between the blogger and the

---

190. Federal Trade Commission, A Brief Overview of the Federal Trade Commission's Investigative and Law Enforcement Authority, last visited July 16, 2013, http://www.ftc.gov/ogc/brfovrvw.shtm.

191. Federal Trade Commission, Guides Concerning the Use of Endorsements and Testimonials in Advertising, 16 CFR § 255, last visited July 16, 2013, http://www.ftc.gov/os/2009/10/091005revisedendorsementguides.pdf.

192. Id.

company, including whether the blogger offered to write a review in exchange for free products or whether the company provided it without an invitation from the blogger. If the company sent the product without an invitation, I suspect the FTC considers whether the company informed the potential reviewer about his obligation to disclose his relationship with the company. I also suspect the FTC considers both parties' ability to pay the fine and which party's behavior needs to change—the blogger who might be soliciting companies for free products or the company who is sending out free products with the hope or expectation that they will be reviewed.

An effective way to comply with this rule is always to be truthful and accurate when reviewing products and to put a disclaimer on every blog post where you are paid for your opinion or receive a product for free.[193] If you blog about products and services where commenters might be compensated for sharing their opinions, you might want to put a notice on your blog that reminds your readers that they must disclose any relationships they have with any product advertisers or sellers in their comments. It would be helpful if software designers who create blogging platforms like WordPress could include in their software a reminder that commenters must disclose any relationships they have with advertisers and sellers.

---

193. "Blog Disclaimer As Per The New FTC Guidelines," *John Jonas*, last visited July 16, 2013, http://www.jonasblog.com/blog-disclaimer-as-per-the-new-ftc-guidelines.

IN SUMMARY

- Review your state's ethical rules regarding advertisements and solicitation, and make sure your blog is in compliance.

- Every legal blog website needs a disclaimer that states that the site only provides general information and that reading the posts does not create a lawyer-client relationship with any reader.

- Federal law requires you to disclose when you are being compensated for providing an endorsement or testimonial. Your testimonials must accurately represent your opinions.

Chapter 18
PROMOTING YOUR BLOG

When you create your blog and release your first post, that is only the beginning. Once you release content, your next step is to promote it. There is little purpose or value in creating and maintaining a blog if no one knows it exists. I will warn you, promoting a blog requires consistent and sometimes significant effort, but it's doable and worthwhile . . . if you do it correctly. The purpose of this chapter is to provide some suggestions about how you can create a successful blog while being aware of the legal and social implications of being a blogger.

BE MINDFUL OF YOUR ETHICAL RULES

As always, review your state's ethical rules regarding advertising before you decide how you want to promote your blog. Most, if not all, of what you can do to promote your blog will be permissible under your state's rules because there is a difference between telling people you've written a post and soliciting people to hire you for legal services. If all you are doing is informing potential readers that you have a blog and some of the topics you cover on it, you're simply sharing information. It shouldn't be classified as advertising.

Just like you don't want to be super "selly-selly" in the writing of your blog posts, you don't want to do it in how you promote your blog. Many people will find this a turn off and it will drive people away from your blog.

Of course, when in doubt, contact your state bar association and ask them how to properly promote your blog within the requirements of your state's rules.

WRITE QUALITY CONTENT

The first rule of having a successful blog is you have to create quality content. You are not going to create a following unless you write posts that are worth reading. All the promotion in the world cannot help you if your work doesn't add value to your readers' lives in some way.

When it comes to creating quality content, think about your readers. Who are they? What are their needs? What questions do they have? Blog posts that provide tips, tricks, and how-to guides are often popular because of their utility. Think about who your readers are and write in their words. If your target audience is non-lawyers, avoid using legalese. This will only confuse them. If you have to use a legal term that is not part of the everyday vernacular, take the time to explain it. One of the best compliments I've received as a legal blogger and public speaker is that I break concepts down for Joe Average people in a way that is effective and doesn't make them "feel stupid."

Remember that a blog post does not have to be long to be effective. In many ways, less is more. If a post is longer than seven hundred words, look for ways to scale it down or break it into two posts. This is one area where "quality has more impact than quantity."[194]

---

194. John Swartz, "30 Ways to Promote Your Blog Posts," June 17, 2013, http://technorati.com/social-media/article/30-ways-to-promote-your-blog/.

CREATE AN ACTION PLAN TO PROMOTE YOUR BLOG

When you are planning and creating your blog, you need to create an action plan that addresses the lifespan of a post. It is helpful to create an editorial calendar where you plan which topics you are going to address in each post. There may be topics that are more pertinent at particular times of the year. For example, a tax lawyer may release posts timed to tax deadlines: in early April, a post on how to file an extension; in September, a follow-up post reminding readers who filed an extension to take care of their taxes; and in December, a post on end-of-year tax planning.

Once you decide how often you are going to release new content, likely weekly or biweekly, be consistent. Release new posts at the same time and the same day of the week. Your readers will come to rely on it and look forward to each new post.

One of the best things my friend did for me when he helped me set up my first blog, The Undeniable Ruth, was making me commit to blogging at least weekly for two years, even when I didn't think I had anything to say. [195] Now, not blogging is not an option for me.

If you are someone who can be excessively busy at times and you worry that you might not have time to blog on a set schedule, create a bank of blog posts with timeless topics. You can have these posts saved in your website ready to go in the event that you don't have time to write a post that week. If you are going to create a blog post bank, make sure you replenish it after you tap into it.

Part of your action plan should be how you're going to promote your blog. You need to decide which forums you're going to use to reach your target audience and how you're going to communicate with them. This sounds fairly straight-forward, but this is one area where it may be prudent to consult marketing professionals on how to do this most effectively.

---

195. *The Undeniable Ruth, supra* note 3.

MAKE YOURSELF EASY TO FIND WITH KEYWORDS

I am not going to delve too deeply into this topic. As a blogger, you should understand the basic benefits of putting tags on your blog posts, whether you do it yourself or have your marketing department or company do it for you.

When you have written a post and are loading it into your website, you have the option to add tags to your work. Without getting super technical, these are words and phrases that, when entered as terms in search engines, are likely to point readers to your post. There are online tools you can use, like Google Adwords, that allow you to search for and examine the words and phrases people are running searches on, so you can add the most prevalent and popular search terms as tags to your post.[196] This will help your target audience find your work through SEO.

For example, I wrote a post about work-made-for-hire contracts that explained how these documents work and who uses them.[197] Some of the tags I added to this post were:

- Arizona business attorney
- Arizona copyright attorney
- Business contract template
- Contract templates
- Copyright attorney
- Copyright infringement
- Copyright license
- Freelance contract
- Freelance contract template

196. Jennine Jacob, "23 Ways to Promote Posts and Increase Your Blog Traffic," *Independent Fashion Bloggers*, last visited July 19, 2013, http://heartifb.com/2013/04/01/23-ways-to-promote-your-blog-posts/.

197. Ruth Carter, How Work Made for Hire Contracts Work, Carter Law Firm, June 13, 2013, http://carterlawaz.com/2013/06/how-work-made-for-hire-contracts-work/.

- Phoenix copyright attorney
- Work made for hire
- Work made for hire contract
- Works made for hire

Additionally, all of my posts on my law firm's blog are tagged with "Ruth Carter" and "Carter Law Firm."

GO TO YOUR READERS

When it comes to promoting your blog, do your research to determine where your target audience is communicating online and promote your work there. It will be easier to communicate with them where they are already hanging out online than to cultivate an audience from scratch.

For example, a business lawyer who focuses on entrepreneurs may make connections with local start-up incubators in real life. When he's interacting with potential clients, he should ask what forums those people use online (Facebook, Twitter, Reddit, LinkedIn, etc.) and create profiles on those sites and actively engage with them there between in-person meetings and events. When the opportunity presents itself, the lawyer can contribute to discussions by referring to posts he's written on the subject matter and provide a link. He can also use the group to create his editorial calendar by asking what questions or topics they would like him to cover.

Keep in mind that it is important to be interesting when talking with people via social media. While it is acceptable to announce when you've released a new post, you don't want to make a generic post like, "Check out my new post" followed by a link that provides no information about the post's topic. Instead, give your posts a snappy introduction, tell people why they should read something or how reading your post will benefit them and then provide a link to the post. Here is an example of a post I made on Twitter announcing a post on my law firm's blog about the benefits of having an operating agreement: "Avoid screaming matches with your business partners in coffee shops—Get an operating agreement: http://bit.ly/166JMZj ." (The bit.ly is a link to the post.) Very few bloggers are popular enough to drive traffic to their sites without telling readers why they should read a particular post.

To see how effectively you are being received in each forum, you may want to use link shorteners like bit.ly, ow.ly, or goo.gl to help track how many times users click on a link. Tracking the number of clicks gives you useful information, such as which topics are interesting to others, which language about a post is effective, and what times of day are best to reach potential readers. Additionally, forums like Facebook, Google+, and Pinterest are very visual; be sure to include an interesting image on your posts to get readers' attention.

Regardless of what social media sites you use to reach potential readers, always remember that the goal of social media is to be a communication forum. Use these sites to talk *with* people, not *at* them, even when you're promoting your blog. Your overall approach to using social media should be more conversational and less like a digital billboard.

Many professionals have profiles on LinkedIn; however, my experience suggests that most people do nothing with their accounts. It's not always the best place to interact with people. Unfortunately, because LinkedIn is the only social media account some people have, it is the only place you can reach them. To maximize the effectiveness of your LinkedIn account, update your LinkedIn status with announcement of each new blog post and include a link. You should also look for LinkedIn groups with members who might be interested in your blog and post discussion items that link to your latest post. LinkedIn users may post comments on group discussions, so be aware of when someone comments and respond when appropriate. Always look for opportunities to interact with others regarding your blog topics. It's a great way to build rapport and relationships with others.

You should also make it easy for your readers to share your posts with others through social media. If you have a WordPress site, you can add a plug-in to your site that allows readers to share your work on popular social media platforms such as Facebook, Twitter and LinkedIn, and to e-mail someone a link to your post. You may also want to create a blog subscription option on your website. Whenever you release a new post, your subscribers will get an e-mail containing your latest post. If you have an electronic newsletter, you may want to include a section of links to your blog (providing an excerpt from a post with a link so recipients can read the rest of the post can also be effective).

INTERACT AND BE RESPONSIVE

I feel like I'm starting to beat a dead horse but I can't stress enough how important it is to be responsive in regard to your blog. Additionally, you want to be attentive to every forum where you post a link to a blog post and respond wherever readers try to interact with you. If you cannot make the commitment to monitoring comments on all the forums where you post a link to your work, perhaps you need to cut down on the number of places you post links. Readers generally dislike it when you appear to ignore them, especially when they ask for feedback in their comments.

Remember that one of the purposes of having a blog is to provide value to your readers. One way to do this is to provide links to other websites that have relevant information. This may also provide an opportunity for you to connect with other website owners. It is also permissible to provide links in your posts to other pertinent pages within your website, especially to places where your readers can learn more about a subject. Your readers will be interested in knowing more about the topic, possibly how you can be of service to them, and other cool things you've done related to a topic.

Additionally, you should read the blogs of others people who write on similar or related topics as you do and leave comments when you have something useful to add to the conversation.[198] If you've written a post on the topic of someone's blog post, you can include it in your comments, but it's best to be thoughtful about your phrasing and not give the impression that you're posting a comment solely to promote yourself. You should be focused on interacting with the writer.

BE CONTROVERSIAL

One way to drive traffic to your website, in addition to creating quality content, is writing controversial posts. Posts that take a strong stance on an issue are more likely to invoke readers to share them with others via e-mail and social media, and leave comments. This is an effective way to generate discussion about your content and possibly inspire other bloggers to write about you and your topic.

When I wrote one of my first controversial blog posts, I got over one thousand hits on my site in a single day, and this was during a time when I was happy to get double-digit readership every day. Apparently other sites were writing about my post and it was driving traffic to my site and inspiring people to leave comments. And some of them were quite cruel and attacked me as much as my ideas. Some of the people were so mean that I called my parents for comfort and support. When I told my Dad, "These people are being mean to me," his response was, "Good." I was taken aback by his reaction but he went on to explain that if everyone agreed with

---

198. Blaise Lucey, "8 Places You Should Promote Your Blog to Get More Readers," *Constant Contact*, last visited July 19, 2013, http://blogs.constantcontact.com/product-blogs/social-media-marketing/promote-blog-more-readers/.

everything I said, then I wasn't pushing the envelope far enough. When people respond with sharp comments, it shows you've struck a chord, and that's usually a good thing.

If you are going to be controversial, you will need to grow a thick skin because people will attack you and probably be meaner to you online than they would be if they were speaking to you in person. You need to be ready for this type of reaction and determine how you want to respond to people who are angry or inflammatory.

USE YOUR NETWORK

One way to increase your blog's popularity is to leverage your network. For example, you can increase the number of comments on a post by inviting specific people to read and comment on it. If you are going to do this, be thoughtful about who you ask to comment on a given post. It needs to be a topic that is applicable to them and you may even want to provide a prompt regarding what type of feedback you're looking for. When you ask someone to comment on your blog, send a personalized invitation to each person; don't send a bulk e-mail. You want each person you invite to feel like they've been singled out to provide a comment.

You can also leverage your network by asking other professionals and bloggers, especially people who have a strong following, to provide quotes or an interview and then featuring their comments on your site. Doing so will provide a fresh perspective or expertise on your website. When you release the post, send the person a thank-you e-mail and provide a link. The person you featured will likely share the post with his network, which will hopefully drive traffic to your site. If people in the featured person's network like your work, they may become new fans and consistent readers of your blog.

Some marketing professionals will suggest you promote your blog by asking your friends and colleagues to promote your work on their social media sites.[199] If you do this, you want to be careful to not look like a jerk who is simply leveraging his network without providing any real value. If you ask someone to promote your work, make sure you have a relationship with that person and that what you're asking him to do makes sense. For instance, if you've established a relationship with the president of an organization and you've written a post that you think would be helpful to the organization's members, sending a link to the president with the suggestion that he pass it along to the members is reasonable.

GUEST BLOGGING FOR OTHERS

I've said before that I am not a fan of letting others write guest posts on my sites; however, it is perfectly fine to write guest posts for other sites. You can use the other site's readership to increase your popularity, and you will boost your credibility by association if you partner with the right site. When you are a guest blogger, select a topic related to a blog post on your website, so you can post a link and possibly drive these readers to your website.

TAKE YOUR INTERACTIONS INTO THE REAL WORLD

One lesson I've learned in networking with people via social media is to bring the interaction into the real world whenever possible. The same is true for your blog. When you meet your readers in person, you will build a stronger connection with them and they will become even bigger fans of your work. When you have readers who are geographically close to you, you can offer to meet one-on-one or let people know if you're attending a networking event or just hanging out at a coffee shop where they are welcome to meet you.

---

199. Jacob, *supra* note 197.

If you are traveling, for example, to attend a conference or meeting, let your readers know where you'll be and when you're open to meeting with them. When I attended the ABA TECHSHOW in Chicago in 2011, I made it a priority to meet with people I had conversed with online if they lived in Chicago or would be attending the conference. You can make your relationships significantly stronger when there is a real-world component.

BE PATIENT BUT PERSISTENT

Unless you are a legal rock star before you start your blog, it will take time to grow your readership. You are not going to have thousands or even hundreds of readers overnight. If you continuously put out quality content, promote your work appropriately, and interact with readers, you will build a solid reputation and fan base. Don't get discouraged; just stick with it and the results will come.

> ### IN SUMMARY
>
> - The first rule for being a successful blogger is to create quality content. No one is going to want to read your work if it's not useful and well written. Write to your target audience's needs.
> - Make it easy for readers to find your work with thoughtful keywords and by posting announcements about new posts on social media forums where your audience is active.
> - Remember that all social media, including blogs, is about interaction. Always respond to comments about your blog wherever they appear— on your site and on other social media forums.
> - It takes time to build a following. Be patient, but persistent.

Chapter 19

I hope this book has helped you understand some of the legal aspects that come with having a blog. Remember that operating your blog legally is only one of your many responsibilities you have if you want to have a successful blog.

The laws that apply to intellectual property and the Internet are constantly evolving, and changes are likely to occur sooner rather than later as it becomes more apparent that the current laws are not sufficient for today's technology and situations. Be sure to stay informed about how the law applies to blogging by following legal blogs and lawyers who can keep you abreast of changes in the law. If you have a specific question about your blog, please consult a social media lawyer.

Additionally, the best practices regarding writing and promoting blogs in general are always being updated. Be sure to stay abreast of the most effective ways to operate your blog by hiring social media professionals—or at least have them in your professional network—and attending education events about blogging and social media marketing.

Everyone who is a legal blogger should be an advocate for legal blogging. This is one area of the legal industry that needs to remain outside the realm of advertising. Likewise, lawyers need to be diligent about not turning their blogs into shameless self-advertising. If you want to bombard your audience with ads, buy a billboard or a make a TV commercial.

Being a blogger is challenging in terms of time, creating quality content, and dealing with the fact that you are opening yourself up to responses from readers—positive and negative. You may feel vulnerable and self-conscious when you put your work on the Internet for all to see. It's hard to read harsh feedback about yourself and your work. I want to share some of the best lessons I've learned from blogging.

HOW TO GROW A THICK SKIN

One thing I've learned about being a blogger is that you have to get a thick skin. When I started posting more controversial blogs, I started getting negative comments on my posts. Sometimes my commenters attacked my work, and sometimes they attacked me directly. It really hurt my feelings. My friend sent me a video clip of comedian Katt Williams that reminded me that there will always be haters and their job is to hate.[200] I try to remember, when people react strongly to my writing, that it's a good thing: something I wrote stirred up something in them. If everyone likes everything you write, you're probably not challenging your readers enough.

When you have haters, don't let their opinions affect you. As the nationally known blogger, podcaster, and author Evo Terra says, "Figure out whose opinions matter to you. Then genuinely do not give a shit what anyone else thinks." This is easier said than done, but these are also words to live by in the blogging world.

---

200. *Katt Williams: The Pimp Chronicles Part 1*, Salient_Media, 2006 (DVD)

BE AUTHENTIC

Another thing I've learned is that it's important to be the same person online as you are in real life. It's disconcerting to meet someone in person and they're who is as nice as can be, and then see them be aggressive and cruel online. If you behave like that, you will lose your credibility. It suggests that you lack integrity. To avoid this problem, a good rule is to never say anything online about someone that you wouldn't say to his face.

When you blog, be mindful that you are building a reputation that may follow you (for better or for worse) for the rest of your career. Every time you add a post, you will be crafting your reputation in the eyes of your readers. If you chose to outsource the writing of some of your blog posts to freelance writers or other lawyers, make sure that they know how to channel your personality and point of view. The same is true if you outsource the marketing of your blog to a marketing team. Their words will become your words.

BE BOLD

You also have a responsibility to your readers, and yourself, to speak honestly and openly. Don't worry if you have trepidation about being bold on your blog. I've been blogging for years and there are still times when I hit *Publish*, and my next thought is "What have I done?" You will get more comfortable with putting yourself out there over time, especially if you are saying things that your readers wish they had the courage to say.

As you create and add to your blog, I encourage you to be bold. Write something that differentiates you from everyone else. Talk about topics about which you have strong opinions. You have a unique voice—use it!

Afterword
FROM THE BLOGGING TRENCHES
—THE NAMBY PAMBY

For those of you who don't know, I'm an anonymous blogger who is absolutely paranoid that my dark, dirty secret is going to escape the Internet and make its way into my partners' hands. The scariest secret that I keep from my coworkers and some friends is what tomfoolery I engage in upon the Internet. Of course, I've done the really stupid thing of having a few too many cocktails and telling someone that I was close to in my office that I am (gasp!) an anonymous law blogger.

Thankfully, none of my drunken confessions to my closest of close work friends have ever come back to bite me in the ass...at least not yet.

As I perused the pages of this book, there were several instances in which I had to stop reading, get up, and walk away because in nearly a decade of being an anonymous blogger, I have done so many stupid things wrong. Granted, I worry about my words getting stolen, but since I don't profit from them, it is not my biggest concern.[201] The biggest concern I have as I continue to blog, tweet, and engage in a certain level of snark is some day being on the receiving end of a lawsuit. I do a fairly decent job of masking the identity of the subjects of my disdain, and I engage all of my intellectual power to (a) write in a humorous manner while (b) being damn sure I never break attorney-client privilege (or any other tenet of professional responsibility).

Worst-case scenario, at least for me, is that my anonymity becomes exposed, resulting in some sort of brouhaha with the state bar. When you tell a joke, someone is bound to be offended because they cannot see the humor in what is being discussed. At the end of the day, I genuinely believe that I do nothing professionally inappropriate (e.g., violate the model rules of professional responsibility, the Supreme Court rules, or the applicable code of civil procedure) with my blogging endeavors[202], and if it ever came to a serious situation, that I would be cleared of any serious wrongdoing. That's not to say that securing a not-guilty would be an inexpensive endeavor, nor does it mean that I would retain my job whilst fighting to clear my name.

As I said, I have not had to worry about this nightmare coming true; however, I did have that one close call that still sends chills through my spine when I think about it.

It was a few years ago that I got an e-mail that shook me to my core. It was a simple notification e-mail from my blog hosting service that I had a new follower that had subscribed to my blog and the e-mail[203] associated with it was for someone who worked for my state bar. I looked at that e-mail fifteen different times before I ran to the firm bathroom and began to dry heave. I was absolutely con-

---

201. Please don't steal my words. Please.

202. Well, maybe I do take the occasional photo inside a courtroom but other than that I am totally innocent!!!

203. Yes, this was to my anonymous e-mail that is not associated with my real name whatsoever.

vinced that I was in a whole pot full of trouble. After I gathered my wits, I started shooting off e-mails and sending messages to my friends throughout the blogosphere "What do I do? What should I do? Do I delete my blog? My Twitter? Can I attempt to scrub my blogging footprint from reality while crawling into a hole?" Clearly these were not exactly reasoned thoughts from someone who the ABA has deemed one of the best legal bloggers for several years running. Yet, this is exactly the thought process I experienced as my worst-case scenario was coming to fruition.

After that sinking feeling in my stomach finally subsided, I emerged from the bathroom still unsure of what action I should take. It was, as I imagine, what a fugitive feels like as the authorities are closing in because I surely did not know what the next several hours were going to entail. I returned to the office and I swear that every time the phone rang I was absolutely convinced it was going to be the state bar asking to have words with me in Guantanamo Bay.

In hindsight, I recognize that I completely overreacted to the situation. In my blogging, I mask the firm I work for[204], I strip clients of identifiable material[205] and, the worst part is I keep the funniest things I experience to myself because those are the stories that would lead to my identification. Nonetheless, I was still on the verge of a full-on panic attack. Thankfully, this did not last for much more than two hours. One of my closest friends and active bloggers convinced me of a simple solution to the mental agony that I was suffering: reach out to the state bar employee who started subscribing to my blog and see what was going on. So that's exactly what I did.

---

204. There are people that aren't entirely sure of my gender or sexual orientation. For what it's worth, I usually do not do anything to disabuse people of any misconception they may have.

205. In blog posts I will change genders, case details, fact scenarios and anything else I can think of to strip the joke of identifiable material. I sure don't make up what I blog about, but I do everything to protect the identities of those involved.

If memory serves, it took me nearly an hour[206] to draft a two-sentence e-mail[207]. Upon hitting send, time stood still as I waited for the response. I made up excuses to partners that wanted me to work on matters for them while my inbox was awaiting a response from the conclave only indentified as "The State Bar." It was probably to my benefit that I did not have any alcohol hidden in my desk because I would have started chugging bourbon if it had been there. The wait did not last much longer and the subscriber responded:

"Hahaha...not at all. We think you're hysterical. Keep up the good work."

There was no laughing on my end when I read this e-mail.

Needless to say, ever since this e-mail exchange, I've been extra vigilant in what I put on the Internet[208] through my blog and Twitter accounts. Yes, I think about this frequently. Yes, I freak about this nightmare scenario frequently. But no, I haven't stopped blogging. All I can say is that thankfully those of you who want to follow the same path that I've gone down now have a handy guide to help you protect yourself when venturing into the unsafe world known as the ENTREENET. Not only has Ruth done a great job capturing common-sense advice, she has also shared legal knowledge to help everyone blog a little smarter. And between you and me, I need all the help I can get when it comes to doing things on the Internet.

You made a great decision by purchasing this book, now stop reading my yammerings and start cramming for the exam on what you've just read.

---

206. No clients were billed in the drafting of this e-mail or as a result of this panic attack.

207. "Hi there. I noticed you started following my blog and I just wanted to make sure that I'm not in any trouble with the powers that be."

208. Disclaimer: The following sentence does not necessarily carry the same meaning when I've been drinking.

Appendix A
STATE AND FEDERAL LAWS RELATED TO BLOGGING

ALABAMA

Anti-SLAPP: None.

Cyberharassment, -bullying, & -stalking: Ala. Code §§ 13A-11-8, 16-28B-1 - 16-28B-9 (2013).

Shield Law: Ala. Code § 12-21-142 (2013).

Trademark Law: Ala. Code §§ 8-2-6 - 8-2-19 (2013).

Ethical Rules for Legal Advertising: Adopted the ABA Model Rules of Professional Conduct (1990).

ALASKA

Anti-SLAPP: None.

Cyberharassment, -bullying, & -stalking: Alaska Stat. §§ 11.41.260, 11.41.270, 14.33.200 - 14.33.250 (2013).

Shield Law: Alaska Stat. §§ 09.25.300-.390 (2013).

Trademark Law: Alaska Stat. §§ 45.50.010-.205 (2013).

Ethical Rules for Legal Advertising: Adopted the ABA Model Rules of Professional Conduct (1993).

ARIZONA

Anti-SLAPP: Ariz. Rev. Stat. §§ 12-751 – 12-752 (2013).

Cyberharassment, -bullying, & -stalking: Ariz. Rev. Stat. §§ 13-2916, 13-2921, 13-2923, 15-341.38 (2013).

Shield Law: Ariz. Rev. Stat. Ann. § 12-2237 (2013). *See* Bartlett v. Superior Court, 722 P.2d 346 (Ariz. Ct. App. 1986); Matera v. Superior Court, 825 P.2d 971 (Ariz. Ct. App. 1992).

Trademark Law: Ariz. Rev. Stat. Ann. §§ 44-1441 - 44-1455 (2013).

Ethical Rules for Legal Advertising: Adopted the ABA Model Rules of Professional Conduct (1984).

ARKANSAS

Anti-SLAPP: Ark. Code Ann. §§ 16-63-501 – 16-63-508 (2013).

Cyberharassment, -bullying, & -stalking: Ark. Code Ann. §§ 5-41-108, 6-18-514, 6-18-1005 (2013).

Shield Law: Ark. Code Ann. § 16-85-510 (2013). *See* Saxton v. Arkansas Gazette Co. 569 S.W.2d 115 (Ark. 1978); In re Grand Jury Subpoena ABC, 947 F.Supp. 1314 (E.D. Ark. 1996).

Trademark Law: Ark. Code Ann. §§ 4-71-201 -218 (2013).

Ethical Rules for Legal Advertising: Adopted the ABA Model Rules of Professional Conduct (1985).

CALIFORNIA

Anti-SLAPP: Cal. Civ. Proc. Code §§ 425.16 – 425.18 (2013).

Cyberharassment, -bullying, & -stalking: Cal. Civil Code § 1708.7 (2013); Cal. Educ. Code §§ 234, 32261-62, 32265, 32270, 32282-83 (2013); Cal. Penal Code §§ 422, 646.9, 653 (2013).

Shield Law: Cal. Evid. Code § 1070 (2013). Miller v. Superior Court, 21 Cal. 4th 883 (1999); Hammarley v. Superior Court, 153 Cal. Rptr. 608 (1979); Mitchell v. Marin County Superior Court, 690 P.2d 625 (Cal. 1984); O'Grady v. Superior Court, 44 Cal. Rptr.3d 72 (2006).

Trademark Law: Cal. Bus. & Prof. Code §§ 14200 et seq. (2013).

Ethical Rules for Legal Advertising: The State Bar of California Rules of Professional Conduct Rule 1-400 (2013).

COLORADO

Anti-SLAPP: None. *See* Protect Our Mountain Environment, Inc. v. Dist. Court, 677 P.2d 1351 (Colo. 1984).

Cyberharassment, -bullying, & -stalking: Colo. Rev. State §§ 18-3-601 - 18-3-602, 22-32-109.1 (2013).

Shield Law: Colo. Rev. Stat. § 13-90-119 (2013).

Trademark Law: Colo. Rev. Stat. §§ 7-70-101 - 7-70-109 (2013).

Ethical Rules for Legal Advertising: Adopted the ABA Model Rules of Professional Conduct (1992).

CONNECTICUT

Anti-SLAPP: None. *See* Field v. Kearns, 682 A.2d 148 (Conn. App. Ct. 1996); Royce v. Willowbrook Cemetery, Inc., No. XO8CV01085694, 2003 WL 431909 (Conn. Super. Ct. Feb. 3,

2003); Arigno v. Murzin, No. CV960474102S, 2001 WL 1265404 (Conn. Super. Ct. Oct. 2, 2001).

Cyberharassment, -bullying, & -stalking: Conn. Gen. Stat. §§ 10-145a, 10-220a, 10-222, 53a-182b, 53a-183 (2013).

Shield Law: Conn. Gen. Stat. § 52-146t (2013).

Trademark Law: Conn. Gen. Stat. §§ 35-11a - 35-11m (2013).

Ethical Rules for Legal Advertising: Adopted the ABA Model Rules of Professional Conduct (1986).

DELAWARE

Anti-SLAPP: Del. Code Ann. tit. 10, §§ 8136 – 8138 (2013).

Cyberharassment, -bullying, & -stalking: Del. Code tit. 11, § 1311, tit 14, §§ 4112D, 4123A (2013).

Shield Law: Del. Code Ann. tit. 10, §§ 4320–26 (2013).

Trademark Law: Del. Code Ann. tit. 6, §§ 3301–3315 (2013).

Ethical Rules for Legal Advertising: Adopted the ABA Model Rules of Professional Conduct (1985).

DISTRICT OF COLUMBIA

Anti-SLAPP: D.C. Code § 18-0351 (2013).

Cyberharassment, -bullying, & -stalking: D.C. Code §§ 2-1535, 22-3133 (2013).

Shield Law: D.C. Code Ann. § 16-4701-04 (2013). *See* Prentice v. McPhilmy, 27 Med. L. Rep. 2377 (D.C. 1999).

Trademark Law: None.

Ethical Rules for Legal Advertising: Adopted the ABA Model Rules of Professional Conduct (1990).

FLORIDA

Anti-SLAPP: Fla. Stat. Ann. § 768.295 (2013).

Cyberharassment, -bullying, & -stalking: Fla. Stat. §§ 784.048, 1006.07, 1006.147 (2013).

Shield Law: Fla. Stat. Ann. § 90.5015 (2013). *See* State v. Davis, 720 So.2d 220 (Fla. 1998); Tribune Co. v. Huffstetler, 489 So2d 722 (Fla. 1986).

Trademark Law: Fla. Stat. Ann. §§ 495.001 - .191 (2013).

Ethical Rules for Legal Advertising: Adopted the ABA Model Rules of Professional Conduct (1986).

GEORGIA

Anti-SLAPP: Ga. Code Ann. § 9-11-11.1 (2013). *See* Berryhill v. Ga. Community Support & Solutions, Inc., 638 S.E.2d 278 (Ga. 2006); Atlanta Humane Society v. Harkins, 603 S.E.2d 289 (Ga. 2004).

Cyberharassment, -bullying, & -stalking: Ga. Code Ann. § 16-5-90, 20-2-145, 20-2-751.4 - 20-2-751.6, 20-2-1181 (2013); Georgia State Board of Education Administrative Rule No. 160-4-8-.15.

Shield Law: Ga. Code Ann. § 24-9-30 (2013). *See* In re Paul, 513 S.E.2d 219 (Ga. 1999).

Trademark Law: Ga. Code Ann. §§ 10-1-440 - 10-1-493 (2013).

Ethical Rules for Legal Advertising: Adopted the ABA Model Rules of Professional Conduct (2000).

HAWAII

Anti-SLAPP: Haw. Rev. Stat. § 634F-1 - 634F-4 (2013).

Cyberharassment, -bullying, & -stalking: Haw. Rev. Stat. §§ 302A-1002, 711-1106 (2013); Hawaii State Board of Education Administrative Rule § 8-19.

Shield Law: None.

Trademark Law: Haw. Rev. Stat. §§ 482-1 - 482-54 (2013).

Ethical Rules for Legal Advertising: Adopted the ABA Model Rules of Professional Conduct (1993).

IDAHO

Anti-SLAPP: None.

Cyberharassment, -bullying, & -stalking: Idaho Code Ann. §§ 18-917a, 18-7905-06, 33-132, 33-205, 33-512 (2013); State Board of Education Administrative Rule § 08.02.03.160.

Shield Law: None. *See* Matter of Contempt of Wright, 700 P.2d 40 (Idaho 1985).

Trademark Law: Idaho Code Ann. §§ 48-501 - 48-518 (2013).

Ethical Rules for Legal Advertising: Adopted the ABA Model Rules of Professional Conduct (1986).

ILLINOIS

Anti-SLAPP: 735 Ill. Comp. Stat. 110/1 - 110/99 (2013). *See* Shoreline Towers Condominium Ass'n v. Gassman, 936 N.E.2d 1198 (Ill. 2010); Sandholm v. Kuecker, 962 N.E.2d 418 (Ill. 2012).

Cyberharassment, -bullying, & -stalking: 105 Ill. Comp. Stat. 5/10-20.14, 5/22-12, 5/27-13.3, 5/27-23.7 (2013); 720 Ill. Comp. Stat. 5/12-7.5, 135/1-2, 135/1-3, 135/2 (2013); 740 Ill. Comp. Stat. 21/10 (2013).

Shield Law: 735 Ill. Comp. Stat. 5/8-901 - 8-909 (2013).

Trademark Law: 765 Ill. Comp. Stat 1036/1 - 999 (2013).

Ethical Rules for Legal Advertising: Adopted the ABA Model Rules of Professional Conduct (1990).

INDIANA

Anti-SLAPP: Ind. Code §§ 34-7-7-1 et seq. (2013).

Cyberharassment, -bullying, & -stalking: Ind. Code §§ 5-2-10.1-2, 5-2-10.1-11, 5-2-10.1-12, 20-33-8-0.2, 20-33-8-13.5, 35-45-2-2 (2013).

Shield Law: Ind. Code §§ 34-46-4-1 - 2 (2013). *See* Jamerson v. Anderson Newspapers, Inc., 469 N.E.2d 1243 (Ind. Ct. App. 1984); In re Indiana Newspapers Inc. v. Junior Achievement of Central Indiana, Inc., No. 49A02-1103-PL-234 (Ind. Ct. App. 2012).

Trademark Law: Ind. Code §§ 24-2-1 et seq. (2013).

Ethical Rules for Legal Advertising: Adopted the ABA Model Rules of Professional Conduct (1986).

IOWA

Anti-SLAPP: None.

Cyberharassment, -bullying, & -stalking: Iowa Code §§ 280.12, 280.28, 708.7 (2013).

Shield Law: None. *See* Waterloo/Cedar Falls Courier v. Hawkeye Community College, 646 N.W.2d 97 (Iowa 2002).

Trademark Law: Iowa Code §§ 548.1 - 548.117 (2013).

Ethical Rules for Legal Advertising: Adopted the ABA Model Rules of Professional Conduct (2005).

KANSAS

Anti-SLAPP: None.

Cyberharassment, -bullying, & -stalking: Kan. Stat. Ann. §§ 21-3438, 72-8256 (2013).

Shield Law: Kan. Stat. Ann. § 60-482 (2013).

Trademark Law: Kan. Stat. Ann. §§ 81-201 - 81-220 (2013).

Ethical Rules for Legal Advertising: Adopted the ABA Model Rules of Professional Conduct (1988).

KENTUCKY

Anti-SLAPP: None.

Cyberharassment, -bullying, & -stalking: Ky. Rev. Stat. §§ 158.148, 158.150, 158.440-41, 158.44, 508.130, 508.150, 525.070, 525.080 (2013).

Shield Law: Ky. Rev. Stat. Ann. § 421.100 (2013).

Trademark Law: Ky. Rev. Stat. Ann. §§ 365.561 - 365.613 (2013).

Ethical Rules for Legal Advertising: Adopted the ABA Model Rules of Professional Conduct (1989).

LOUISIANA

Anti-SLAPP: La. Code Civ. Proc. Ann. Art. 971 (2013). *See* Darden v. Smith, 879 So.2d 390 (La. Ct. App. 2004).

Cyberharassment, -bullying, & -stalking: La. Rev. Stat. Ann. §§ 14:40.2, 14:40.3 14:40.7, 17:280, 17:416.13, 17:416.20 (2013).

Shield Law: La. Rev. Stat. §§ 45:1451-59 (2013). *See* In re Burns, 484 So.2d 658 (La. 1986); In re Grand Jury Proceedings (Ridenhour), 520 So.2d 372 (La. 1988).

Trademark Law: La. Rev. Stat. Ann. §§ 51:211 - 51:300.32 (2013).

Ethical Rules for Legal Advertising: Adopted the ABA Model Rules of Professional Conduct (1986).

MAINE

Anti-SLAPP: Me. Rev. Stat. Ann. tit. 14, § 556 (2013).

Cyberharassment, -bullying, & -stalking: Me. Rev. Stat. Ann. tit. 17-A, § 210A (2013), tit. 20-A §§ 254 subsection 11A, 1001.15H, 6554 (2013).

Shield Law: Me. Rev. Stat. Ann. tit. 16, § 61 (2013).

Trademark Law: Me. Rev. Stat. Ann. tit. 10 § 1521 - 1532 (2013).

Ethical Rules for Legal Advertising: Adopted the ABA Model Rules of Professional Conduct (2009).

MARYLAND

Anti-SLAPP: Md. Code Ann. Cts. & Jud. Proc. § 5-807 (2013). *See* Ugwuonye v. Rotimi, No. PJM 09-658, 2010 WL 3038099 (D. Md. July 30, 2010); Russell v. Krowne, No. DKC 2008-2468, 2010 WL 2765268 (D. Md. July 12, 2010).

Cyberharassment, -bullying, & -stalking: Md. Code. Ann., Crim. Law § 3-805 (2013); Md. Code. Ann., Educ. § 7-424 (2013); Code of Maryland State Board of Education Regulation § 13A.01.04.03.

Shield Law: Md. Cts. & Jud. Proc. Code Ann. § 9-112 (2013). *See* Bilney v. Evening Star Newspaper Co., 406 A.2d 652 (Md. Ct. App. 1979).

Trademark Law: Md. Code Ann., Bus. Reg §§ 1-401 et seq. (2013).

Ethical Rules for Legal Advertising: Adopted the ABA Model Rules of Professional Conduct (1986).

MASSACHUSETTS

Anti-SLAPP: Mass. Gen. Laws Ann. ch. 231 § 59H (2013). See Fustolo v. Hollander, 920 N.E.2d 837 (Mass. 2010); Stuborn Ltd. P'ship v. Bernstein, 245 F. Supp. 2d 312 (D. Mass. 2003); Fabre v. Walton, 802 N.E.2d 1030 (Mass. 2004).

Cyberharassment, -bullying, & -stalking: Mass. Gen. Laws ch. 69 § 1D; ch. 71 §§ 37H, 37O, 93, ch. 265 §§ 43, 43A; ch. 269 § 14A (2013).

Shield Law: None. *See* Sinnott v. Boston Retirement Board, 524 N.E.2d 100 (Mass. 1988), cert. denied, 109 S.Ct. 528 (1988).

Trademark Law: 950 Mass. Code Regs. 62.01 - 62.21(2013).

Ethical Rules for Legal Advertising: Adopted the ABA Model Rules of Professional Conduct (1997).

MICHIGAN

Anti-SLAPP: None.

Cyberharassment, -bullying, & -stalking: Mich. Comp. Laws. §§ 380.1310b, 750.411h, 750.411i, 750.411s (2013).

Shield Law: Mich. Comp. Laws §§ 767.5a, 767A.6 (2013). *See* Marketos v. American Employers Ins. Co., 460 N.W.2d 272 (Mich. Ct. App. 1990).

Trademark Law: Mich. Comp. Laws §§ 429.31 - 429.46 (2013).

Ethical Rules for Legal Advertising: Adopted the ABA Model Rules of Professional Conduct (1988).

MINNESOTA

Anti-SLAPP: Minn. Stat. §§ 554.01 – 554.05 (2013). Freeman v. Swift, 776 N.W.2d 485 (Minn. Ct. App. 2009); Special Force Ministries v. WCCO Television, 576 N.W.2d 746 (Minn. 1998). **Cyberharassment, -bullying, & -stalking:** Minn. Stat. §§ 121A.0695, 609.749, 609.795 (2013).

Shield Law: Minn. Stat. Ann. §§ 595.021-.025 (2013). See Arial Burials, Inc. v. Minneapolis Star and Tribune Co., 8 Med. L. Rep. 1653 (Minn. Dist. Ct. 1982); Cohen v. Cowels Media,479 N.W.2d 387 (Minn. 1992); State v. Turner, 550 N.W.2d 622 (Minn. 1999); Weinberger v. Maplewood Review, 648 N.W.2d 249 (Minn. App. 2002).

Trademark Law: Minn. Stat. Ann. §§ 333.001 et seq. (2013).

Ethical Rules for Legal Advertising: Adopted the ABA Model Rules of Professional Conduct (1985).

MISSISSIPPI

Anti-SLAPP: None.

Cyberharassment, -bullying, & -stalking: Miss. Code Ann. §§ 37-11-20, 37-11-54, 37-11-67, 37-11-69, 97-3-107, 97-29-45, 97-45-15, 97-45-17 (2013).

Shield Law: None. See Brinston v. Dunn, 919 F. Supp. 240 (S.D. Miss. 1996).

Trademark Law: Miss. Code. Ann. §§ 75-25-1 - 75-25-33 (2013).

Ethical Rules for Legal Advertising: Adopted the ABA Model Rules of Professional Conduct (1987).

MISSOURI

Anti-SLAPP: Mo. Rev. Stat. § 537.528 (2013). Moschenross v. St. Louis County, 188 S.W.3d 13 (Mo. Ct. App. 2006).

Cyberharassment, -bullying, & -stalking: Mo. Rev. Stat. §§ 160.261, 160.775, 167.117, 565.090, 565.225 (2013).

Shield Law: None. See *State ex. rel.* Classic III, Inc. v. Ely, 954 S.W.2d 650 (Mo. Ct. App. W.D. 1997).

Trademark Law: Mo. Rev. Stat. §§ 417.005 - 417.066 (2013).

Ethical Rules for Legal Advertising: Adopted the ABA Model Rules of Professional Conduct (1985).

MONTANA

Anti-SLAPP: None.

Cyberharassment, -bullying, & -stalking: Mont. Code Ann. §§ 45-5-220, 45-8-213 (2013).

Shield Law: Mont. Code Ann. §§ 26-1-901 - 26-1-903 (2013).

Trademark Law: Mont. Code Ann. §§ 30-13-301 - 30-13-341 (2013).

Ethical Rules for Legal Advertising: Adopted the ABA Model Rules of Professional Conduct (1985).

NEBRASKA

Anti-SLAPP: Neb. Rev. Stat. §§ 25-21,241 – 25-21,246 (2013).

Cyberharassment, -bullying, & -stalking: Neb. Rev. Stat. §§ 28-311.02, 79-267, 79-2,137 (2013).

Shield Law: Neb. Rev. Stat. §§ 20-144 - 47 (2013).

Trademark Law: Neb. Rev. Stat. §§ 87-126 - 87-306 (2013).

Ethical Rules for Legal Advertising: Adopted the ABA Model Rules of Professional Conduct (2005).

NEVADA

Anti-SLAPP: Nev. Rev. Stat. §§ 41.635 – 41.670 (2013).

Cyberharassment, -bullying, & -stalking: Nev. Rev. Stat. §§ 200.575, 200.725, 385.34692, 385.347, 388.121 - .125, 388.129, 388.132, 388.1325, 388.1327, 388.133 - .134, 388.1342 - .1344, 388.135 - .1353, 388.1355, 388.136 - .137, 388.139, 389.520, 392.915 (2013).

Shield Law: Nev. Rev. Stat. § 49.275 (2013).

Trademark Law: Nev. Rev. Stat. §§ 600.050 - 600.120 (2013).

Ethical Rules for Legal Advertising: Adopted the ABA Model Rules of Professional Conduct (1986).

NEW HAMPSHIRE

Anti-SLAPP: None.

Cyberharassment, -bullying, & -stalking: N.H. Rev. Stat. Ann. §§ 193-F:1-10, 644:4 (2013)

Shield Law: None. *See* Opinion of the Justices, 373 A.2d 644 (N.H. 1977); New Hampshire v. Siel, 444 A.2d 499 (N.H. 1982).

Trademark Law: N.H. Rev. Stat. Ann. §§ 350-A:1 - 350-A:15 (2013).

Ethical Rules for Legal Advertising: Adopted the ABA Model Rules of Professional Conduct (1986).

NEW JERSEY

Anti-SLAPP: None.

Cyberharassment, -bullying, & -stalking: N.J. Rev. Stat. §§ 2C:12-10, 2C: 12-10.1, 18A:37-13 - 37-32 (2013).

Shield Law: N.J. Rev. Stat. §§ 2A:84A-21 - 2A:84A-21.9, 2A:84A-29 (2013). See In re Schuman, 552 A. 2d 602 (N.J. 1989); Too Much Media, LLC v. Hale, 20 A. 3d 364 (N.J. 2011).

Trademark Law: N.J. Rev. Stat. §§ 56:3-13.1a - 56:3-13.22 (2013).

Ethical Rules for Legal Advertising: Adopted the ABA Model Rules of Professional Conduct (1984).

NEW MEXICO

Anti-SLAPP: N.M. Stat. §§ 38-2-9.1 – 38-2-9.2 (2013).

Cyberharassment, -bullying, & -stalking: N.M. Stat. § 30-3A-3 (2013); N.M. Education Code § 22-2-21 (2013); N.M. Administrative Code §§ 6.12.7.1 - 6.12.7.8 (2013).

Shield Law: N.M. Sup. Ct. R. § 11-514 (2013).

Trademark Law: N.M. Stat. §§ 57-3B-1 - 57-3B-17 (2013).

Ethical Rules for Legal Advertising: Adopted the ABA Model Rules of Professional Conduct (1986).

NEW YORK

Anti-SLAPP: N.Y. C.P.L.R. 70-a, 76-a, 3211 (2013). *See* Long Island Ass'n for AIDS Care v. Greene, 702 N.Y.S.2d 914 (N.Y. App. Div. 2000); Hariri v. Amper, 854 N.Y.S.2d 126 (N.Y. App. Div. 2008).

Cyberharassment, -bullying, & -stalking: N.Y. Educ. Law §§ 10-18, 814 (2013); N.Y. Penal Law § 240.30 (2013).

Shield Law: N.Y. Civ. Rights Law § 79-H (2013). See New York v. Hennessey, 13 Med. L. Rep. 1109 (N.Y. Dist. Ct. 1986); O'Neill v. Oakgrove Const., Inc., 71 N.Y.2d 524 (1988).

Trademark Law: N.Y. Gen. Bus. Law § 360 (2013).

Ethical Rules for Legal Advertising: Adopted the ABA Model Rules of Professional Conduct (2008).

NORTH CAROLINA

Anti-SLAPP: None.

Cyberharassment, -bullying, & -stalking: N.C. Gen. Stat. §§ 14-196(b), 14-196.3, 14-458.1, 115C-407.15 - 115C-407.18 (2013).

Shield Law: N.C. Gen. Stat. § 8-53.11 (2013). *See* In re Owens, 496 SE 2d 592 (N.C. Ct. App. 1998).

Trademark Law: N.C. Gen. Stat. §§ 80-1- 80-66 (2013).

Ethical Rules for Legal Advertising: Adopted the ABA Model Rules of Professional Conduct (1985).

NORTH DAKOTA

Anti-SLAPP: None.

Cyberharassment, -bullying, & -stalking: N.D. Cent. Code §§ 12.1-17-07, 15.1-19-17 - 15.1-19-22 (2013).

Shield Law: N.D. Cent. Code § 31-01-06.2 (2013). *See* Grand Folks Herald v. District Court, 322 N.W.2d 850 (N.D. 1982).

Trademark Law: N.D. Cent. Code §§ 47-22-01 - 47-22-13 (2013).

Ethical Rules for Legal Advertising: Adopted the ABA Model Rules of Professional Conduct (1987).

OHIO

Anti-SLAPP: None.

Cyberharassment, -bullying, & -stalking: Ohio Rev. Code Ann. §§ 2903.211, 2913.01, 2917.21, 3301.22, 3313.6667 - .667 (2013)

Shield Law: Ohio Rev. Code Ann. §§ 2739.04, 2739.12 (2013). *See* State v. Geis, 441 N.E.2d 803 (Ohio 1981); Fawley v. Quirk, 11 Med. L. Rep. 2336 (Ohio Ct. App. 1985); In re Grand Jury Proceedings, 749 N.E.2d 325 (Ohio Ct. App. 1999); Svoboda v. Clear Channel Communications, Inc., 2004 Ohio 894 (6th Dist. Ct. App. 2004).

Trademark Law: Ohio Rev. Code Ann. §§ 1329.01 et seq. (2013).

Ethical Rules for Legal Advertising: Adopted the ABA Model Rules of Professional Conduct (2006).

OKLAHOMA

Anti-SLAPP: Okla. Stat. tit. 12, § 1443.1 (2013).

Cyberharassment, -bullying, & -stalking: Okla. Stat. tit. 21 §§ 1172-73; tit 70, §§ 24-100.2 - 100.5 (2013).

Shield Law: Okla. Stat. tit. 12, § 2506 (2013). *See* Taylor v. Miskovsky, 640 P.2d 959 (Okla. 1981).

Trademark Law: Okla. Stat. tit. 78, §§ 21 et seq. (2013).

Ethical Rules for Legal Advertising: Adopted the ABA Model Rules of Professional Conduct (1988).

OREGON

Anti-SLAPP: Or. Rev. Stat. §§ 31.150 et seq. (2013).

Cyberharassment, -bullying, & -stalking: Or. Rev. Stat. §§ 163.730 - .732, 166.065, 339.351 - .364 (2013).

Shield Law: Or. Rev. Stat. §§ 44.510-44.540 (2013).

Trademark Law: Or. Rev. Stat. §§ 647.005 - 647.730 (2011).

Ethical Rules for Legal Advertising: Adopted the ABA Model Rules of Professional Conduct (2005).

PENNSYLVANIA

Anti-SLAPP: 27 Pa. Cons. Stat. §§ 7707, 8301 – 8303 (2013). *See* Penllyn Greene Assocs., L.P. v. Clouser, 890 A.2d 424 (Pa. Commw. Ct. 2005).

Cyberharassment, -bullying, & -stalking: 18 Pa. Cons. Stat. §§ 2709-2709.1 (2013); 24 Pa. Cons. Stat. § 13-1303.1A (2013).

Shield Law: 42 Pa. Cons. Stat. Ann. § 5942(a) (2013). *See* Davis v. Glanton, 705 A. 2d 879 (Pa. Super. Ct. 1997); Commonwealth v. Tyson, 800 A.2d 327 (Pa. Super. Ct. 2002); Com. v. Bowden, 838 A. 2d 740 (Pa. 2003); Castellani v. Scranton Times, LP, 956 A.2d 937 (Pa. 2008).

Trademark Law: 54 Pa. Cons. Stat. §§ 1101 - 1126 (2013).

Ethical Rules for Legal Advertising: Adopted the ABA Model Rules of Professional Conduct (1987).

RHODE ISLAND

Anti-SLAPP: R.I. Gen. Laws §§ 9-33-1 – 9-33-4 (2013).

Cyberharassment, -bullying, & -stalking: R.I. Gen. Laws §§ 11-52-4.2, 16-21-21, 16-21-24, 16-21-33 - 34 (2013).

Shield Law: R.I. Gen. Law §§ 9-19.1-1 et seq. (2013). *See* Outlet Communications, Inc. v. State, 588 A.2d 1050 (R.I. 1991).

Trademark Law: R.I. Gen. Laws §§ 6-2-1 - 6-2-16 (2013).

Ethical Rules for Legal Advertising: Adopted the ABA Model Rules of Professional Conduct (1988).

SOUTH CAROLINA

Anti-SLAPP: None.

Cyberharassment, -bullying, & -stalking: S.C. Code Ann. §§ 16-3-1700, 16-17-430, 59-63-110 - 150, 59-63-425 (2013).

Shield Law: S.C. Code Ann. § 19-11-100 (2013). See Matter of Decker 471 S.E.2d 462 (S.C. 1995).

Trademark Law: S.C. Code Ann. §§ 39-15-10 et seq. (2013).

Ethical Rules for Legal Advertising: Adopted the ABA Model Rules of Professional Conduct (1990).

SOUTH DAKOTA

Anti-SLAPP: None.

Cyberharassment, -bullying, & -stalking: S.D. Cod. Laws §§ 13-32-14 - 19, 22-19A-1, 49-31-31 (2013).

Shield Law: None. *See* Hopewell v. Midcontinent Broadcasting Corporation, 538 N.W.2d 780 (S.D. 1995).

Trademark Law: S.D. Cod. Laws §§ 37-6-1 - 37-6-32 (2013).

Ethical Rules for Legal Advertising: Adopted the ABA Model Rules of Professional Conduct (1987).

TENNESSEE

Anti-SLAPP: Tenn. Code Ann. §§ 4-21-1001 -21-1004 (2013).

Cyberharassment, -bullying, & -stalking: Tenn. Code Ann. §§ 39-17-308, 39-17-315, 49-6-1014 - 1019 (2013).

Shield Law: Tenn. Code Ann. § 24-1-208 (2013). *See* Austin v. Memphis Publishing Co., 655 S.W.2d 146 (Tenn. 1983); Tennessee v. Curriden, 14 Med. L. Rep. 1797 (Tenn. 1987); State v. Kendrick, 178 S.W.3d 734 (Tenn. Crim. App. 2005).

Trademark Law: Tenn. Code Ann. §§ 47-25-501 - 47-25-518 (2013).

Ethical Rules for Legal Advertising: Adopted the ABA Model Rules of Professional Conduct (2002).

TEXAS

Anti-SLAPP: Tex. Civ. Prac. & Rem. Code Ann. §§ 27.001 et seq. (2013).

Cyberharassment, -bullying, & -stalking: Tex. Penal Code Ann. § 33.07 (2013); Tex. Educ. Code Ann. §§ 21.451, 25.0342, 28.002, 37.001, 37.0832, 37.083a, 37.123-.24, 37.217 (2013).

Shield Law: Tex. Civ. Prac. & Rem., Code Ann. §§ 22.021 - 22.027 (2013); Tex Code Crim. Ann. § 38.11 (2013). *See* Channel Two Television v. Dickerson, 725 S.W.2d 470 (Tex. App. 1987); Campbell v. Klevenhagen, 760 F.Supp. 1206 (S.D. Tex. 1991); In re Union Pacific R. Co., 6 S.W.3d 310 (Tex. App. 1999).

Trademark Law: Tex. Bus. & Com. Code Ann. §§ 16.001 et seq. (2013).

Ethical Rules for Legal Advertising: Adopted the ABA Model Rules of Professional Conduct (1989).

UTAH

Anti-SLAPP: Utah Code Ann. §§ 78B-6-1401 – 1405 (2013).

Cyberharassment, -bullying, & -stalking: Utah Code Ann. §§ 53A-11-904, 53A-11a-101 - 102, 53A-11a-201 - 202,

53A-11a-301 - 302, 53A-11a-401 - 402, 76-5-106.5, 76-9-201 (2013); Utah State Board of Education Policy §§ R227-609, R227-613.

Shield Law: Utah R. Evid. Rule 509 (2013). *See* Silkwood v. Kerr-McGee Corp., 563 F.2d 433 (10th Cir. 1977).

Trademark Law: Utah Code Ann. §§ 70-3a-101 - 70-3a-502 (2013).

Ethical Rules for Legal Advertising: Adopted the ABA Model Rules of Professional Conduct (1987).

VERMONT

Anti-SLAPP: Vt. Stat. Ann. tit. 12, § 1041 (2013).

Cyberharassment, -bullying, & -stalking: Vt. Stat. Ann. tit. 13 §§ 1027, 1061 - 1063; tit. §§ 11, 14, 570-570c,1161a (2013).

Shield Law: None. *See* State v. St. Peter, 315 A.2d 254 (Vt. 1974); In re Inquest Subpoena (WCAX), 890 A.2d 1240 (Vt. 2005); Spooner v. Town of Topsham, 937 A.2d 641 (Vt. 2007).

Trademark Law: Vt. Stat. Ann. tit. 9 §§ 2521 - 2575 (2013).

Ethical Rules for Legal Advertising: Adopted the ABA Model Rules of Professional Conduct (1999).

VIRGINIA

Anti-SLAPP: None.

Cyberharassment, -bullying, & -stalking: Va. Code Ann. §§ 8.01-220.1:2, 9.1-184, 18.2-60, 18.2-152.7:1, 22.1-208.01, 22.1-279.3:1, 22.1-279.6 (2013).

Shield Law: None. *See* Brown v. Commonwealth of Virginia, 204 S.E.2d 429 (Va. 1974), cert. denied, Brown v. Virginia, 419 U.S.

966 (1974); Clemente v. Clemente, 56 Va. Cir. 530 (Arlington 2001).

Trademark Law: Va. Code Ann. §§ 59.1-92.1 - 59.1-92.22 (2013).

Ethical Rules for Legal Advertising: Adopted the ABA Model Rules of Professional Conduct (1999).

WASHINGTON

Anti-SLAPP: Wash. Rev. Code §§ 4.24.500-525 (2013).

Cyberharassment, -bullying, & -stalking: Wash. Rev. Code §§ 9.61.260, 9A.36.080, 9A.46.020, 9A.46.110, 10.14.020, 28A.300.285, 28A.300.2851, 28A.660.480, 43.06B.060 (2013).

Shield Law: Wash. Rev. Code § 5.68.010 (2013). *See* Senear v. Daily Journal-American, 641 P.2d 1180 (Wash. 1982); In the Matter of the Request of Plaintiff Alfredo Azule et al., 29 Med. L. Rep. 1414 (Wash. App. 2001).

Trademark Law: Wash. Rev. Code §§ 19.77.010 - 19.77.940 (2013).

Ethical Rules for Legal Advertising: Adopted the ABA Model Rules of Professional Conduct (1985).

WEST VIRGINIA

Anti-SLAPP: None. *See Harris v. Adkins*, 432 S.E.2d 549 (W. Va. 1993); Graham v. Beverage, 566 SE 2d 603 (W. Va. 2002).

Cyberharassment, -bullying, & -stalking: W. Va. Code § 18-2-7B, 18-2C-1 - 6, 18A-5-1, 18A-5-1c, 61-3C-14a (2013).

Shield Law: W. Va. Code § 57-3-10 (2013). *See* State ex rel. Hudok v. Henry, 389 S.E.2d 188 (W. Va. 1989); State ex rel. Charleston Mail v. Ranson, 488 S.E.2d 5 (W. Va. 1997).

Trademark Law: W. Va. Code §§ 47-2-1 - 47-2-19 (2012).

Ethical Rules for Legal Advertising: Adopted the ABA Model Rules of Professional Conduct (1988).

WISCONSIN

Anti-SLAPP: None.

Cyberharassment, -bullying, & -stalking: Wis. Stat. §§ 118.13, 118.46, 947.0125 (2013).

Shield Law: Wis. Stat. § 885.14 (2013). *See* State v. Zelenka, 387 NW 2d 55 (Wis. 1986);

Kurzynski v. Spaeth, 538 N.W.2d 554 (Wis. Ct. App. 1995).

Trademark Law: Wis. Stat. §§ 132.001 - 132.25 (2013).

Ethical Rules for Legal Advertising: Adopted the ABA Model Rules of Professional Conduct (1987).

WYOMING

Anti-SLAPP: None.

Cyberharassment, -bullying, & -stalking: Wyo. Stat. Ann. §§ 6-2-506, 21-4-311 - 315 (2013).

Shield Law: None. *See* Silkwood v. Kerr-McGee Corp., 563 F.2d 433 (10th Cir. 1977).

Trademark Law: Wyo. Stat. Ann. §§ 40-1-101 - 40-1-113 (2013).

Ethical Rules for Legal Advertising: Adopted the ABA Model Rules of Professional Conduct (1986).

FEDERAL LAWS

Children's Online Privacy Protection Act (COPPA) of 1998: 15 U.S.C. §§ 6501–6506 (2013).

Communications Decency Act of 1996, Sec. 230: 47 U.S.C. § 230 (2012).

Controlling the Assault of Non-Solicited Pornography and Marketing (CAN-SPAM) Act of 2003: 15 U.S.C. §§ 7701-7713 (2012).

Copyright Act of 1976: 17 U.S.C. §§ 101-1332 (2012).

E-government Act of 2002: 44 U.S.C. § 101-4101 (2012).

Electronic Communications Privacy Act (ECPA) of 1986: 18 U.S.C. §§ 2510-2522 (2012).

Federal Information Security Management Act (FISMA) of 2002: 44 U.S.C. §§ 3541-3549 (2012).

Freedom of Information Act (FOIA) of 1966: 5 U.S.C. § 552 (2012).

Lanham (Trademark) Act: 15 U.S.C. §§ 1501-1141n (2012).

National Labor Relations Act (NLRA) of 1935: 29 U.S.C. §§ 151–169 (2012).

Privacy Protection Act (PPA) of 1980: 42 U.S.C. §§ 2000aa-2000aa12 (2012).

Appendix B
ONLINE RESOURCES RELATED TO BLOGGING

Existing Federal Privacy Laws, Center for Democracy and Technology: https://www.cdt.org/privacy/guide/protect/laws.php

Model Rules of Professional Conduct, American Bar Association: http://www.americanbar.org/groups/professional_responsibility/publications/model_rules_of_professional_conduct/model_rules_of_professional_conduct_table_of_contents.html.

Online Defamation Law, Electronic Frontier Foundation: https://www.eff.org/issues/bloggers/legal/liability/defamation.

Privacy, Electronic Frontier Foundation: https://www.eff.org/issues/bloggers/legal/liability/privacy.

Public Participation Project: http://www.anti-slapp.org/your-states-free-speech-protection/

Reporters Committee for Freedom of the Press State-by-State Guide: http://www.rcfp.org/slapp-stick-fighting-frivolous-lawsuits-against-journalists/state-state-guide

The Reporter's Privilege, Reporters Committee for Freedom of the Press: http://www.rcfp.org/reporters-privilege

State Anti-Bullying Laws and Policies, Stopbullying.gov: http://www.stopbullying.gov/laws.

State-by-State Guide to the Reporter's Privilege for Student Media, Student Press Law Center: http://www.splc.org/knowyourrights/legalresearch.asp?id=60

State Cyberbullying Laws, June 2013: http://cyberbullying.us/Bullying_and_Cyberbullying_Laws.pdf

State Law: Defamation, Digital Media Law Project: http://www.dmlp.org/legal-guide/state-law-defamation

State Shield Laws, Bloggers Beware: Don't Let Others Define You: http://blogs.law.harvard.edu/beware/background-on-the-shield-bill/state-shield-laws/

State Trademark Information Links, United States Patent and Trademark Office: http://www.uspto.gov/trademarks/process/State_Trademark_Links.jsp.

Appendix C

ADDITIONAL BOOKS ON BLOGGING AND SOCIAL MEDIA MARKETING

All Marketers Are Liars: The Underground Classic That Explains How Marketing Really Works—and Why Authenticity Is the Best Marketing of All — Seth Godin, Portfolio Trade, 2012.

Blogging in One Hour for Lawyers — Ernie Svenson, American Bar Association Law Practice Management Section, 2012.

Contagious: Why Things Catch On — Jonah Berger, Simon & Schuster, 2013.

Content Rules: How to Create Killer Blogs, Podcasts, Videos, Ebooks, Webinars (and More) That Engage Customers and Ignite Your Business — Ann Handley and C.C. Chapman, Wiley, 2012.

Duct Tape Marketing Marketing Revised & Updated: The World's Most Practical Small Business Marketing Guide — John Jantsch, Thomas Nelson, 2011.

Jab, Jab, Jab, Right Hook: How to Tell Your Story in a Noisy, Social World — Gary Vaynerchuk, HarperBusiness, 2013.

ProBlogger: Secrets for Blogging Your Way to a Six-Figure Income — Darren Rowse and Chris Garrett, Wiley, 2012.

Reinventing Professional Services: Building Your Business in the Digital Marketplace — Ari Kaplan, Wiley, 2011.

Smarter, Faster, Cheaper: Non-Boring, Fluff-Free Strategies for Marketing and Promoting Your Business — David Siteman Garland, Wiley, 2010.

The Impact Equation: Are You Making Things Happen or Just Making Noise? — Chris Brogan and Julien Smith, Portfolio Hardcover, 2012.

The NOW Revolution: 7 Shifts to Make Your Business Faster, Smarter and More Social — Jay Baer and Amber Naslund, Wiley, 2011.

The Power of Unpopular: A Guide to Building Your Brand for the Audience Who Will Love You (and why no one else matters) — Erika Napoletano, Wiley, 2012.

The Referral Engine: Teaching Your Business to Market Itself — John Jantsch, Portfolio Trade, 2012.

The Thank You Economy — Gary Vaynerchuk, HarperCollins, 2013.

Youtility: Why Smart Marketing is about Help, Not Hype — Jay Baer, Portfolio Hardcover, 2013

Index

A

action plan for blog promotion, 159

actual damages for copyright
infringement, 37–38

actual malice, 80, 82
defense against, 84–85
in false light claims, 89
in intentional infliction of emotional
distress claims, 93

Acuff-Rose Music, Inc., 27

Adecco, 98

advertising
vs. blogging, 169–170
of blog vs. lawyer services, 157–158
rules on, 141–145

advertising disclaimers, 143, 145

advice requests, responding to, 149–150

affirmative defenses, fair use doctrine,
25–30

American Bar Association
Model Rules of Professional Conduct
on advertising and solicitation,
142–144
Top 100 Law Blawgs, 6

analytics, website
click tracking, 162
monitoring, 45

anonymous bloggers, 6–7

anonymity, maintaining, 4
identity, protecting in defamation
cases, 78–79
IP address tracking and, 7
legal actions against, 10
Namby Pamby, 6, 173–176
registering with U.S. Copyright
Office, 40–41

anonymous information sources,
protecting identity of, 61–64

anonymous persons in defamation cases,
78–79

anonymous speech, First Amendment
protections, 6–7

anti-SLAPP laws, 12
listed by state, 177–198

Around the World in Eighty Jobs blog, 98

arrests
because of blog posts, 119–123
blogs as evidence, 122–123

assault laws, 119–120

at-will employees, firing of, 111–112

audience. See readers; readership

authenticity of bloggers, 171

Avvo, 77
recommendations, rules on, 152

B

Bankruptcy Corruption blog, 107–108
bar complaints, 10
Barr, Turner, 98
benefits of blogging, 129–139
    credibility, building, 130–131
    expertise, establishing, 130–131
    personality, sharing, 133–134
    relationship building, 135
    reputation, leveraging, 131–132
bit.ly, 162
BL1Y, 6
BL1Y: The Life and Adventures of a
    Defunct Big Law Associate blog, 6
bloggers
    authenticity of, 130–131, 171
    boldness of, 171
    as employees, 54–55, 57–58
    guest bloggers, 69–73, 166
    independent contractors, 55–58
    interacting with other bloggers, 164
    online behavior, 111–123
    qualification as journalists, 62, 64
    quoting other bloggers, 165
    reputation of, 115, 131–132, 134,
        137, 171
    shield law protection of, 63
blogging
    vs. advertising, 169–170
    anonymity in, 6–7
    arrests resulting from, 119–123
    benefits of, 129–139
    best practices, keeping up with, 169
    books on, 203–204
    commitment to, 136–137
    death by, 125–128
    employer limits on, 111
    ethical issues of, 141–155
    getting fired because of, 111–118
    laws related to, 169, 177–199
    online resources on, 201–202
    revenue from, 132
    rule of thumb for, 3–4
    schedule for, 136–137, 159
    thick skin for, 170
blog posts. *See also* content
    banking, 159
    images with, 136, 162

    permissible posts, 6
    schedule for, 136–137, 159
    sharing, 163
    tagging with keywords, 160–161
blogs
    analyzing popularity, 162
    categorizing for copyright
        registration, 33–34
    as commercial speech, 142–143
    company blogs, 112
    as conversations with readers, 65–66,
        135, 162, 164
    as copyrightable works, 16–17,
        33–41
    Creative Commons licensing, 40
    crimes committed via, 119–123,
        125–127
    economic motivations for, 143
    as evidence in arrests, 122–123
    as forum for discussion, 5, 129
    free information on, 137–138
    geographic reach of, 105–106
    interactive features, 143–144
    interviews on, 73
    jurisdiction over, 127–128
    as marketing mechanisms, 129, 138
    negative results of, 115
    off-limits personal topics, 134
    ownership of, 2
    promotion of, 157–167
    public nature of, 117
    quality content for, 129, 137
    registering with U.S. Copyright
        Office, 33–41
    responsiveness of, 163–164
    subscription options, 163
    target audience, 3, 135
    terms of service, 68–69, 72–73,
        108–109
    timeliness of, 131
    topics, choosing, 150
    trademark problems, 100–103
    value provision with, 131
Bloomsbury Publishing, 18
Blumberg, Elliot, 77–78
books on blogging and social media,
    203–204
Brave New Films 501(c)(4) v. Weiner, 47

breach of contract with anonymous
    sources, 62, 64
bullying, 121–122
Burger King, 97
Burnside, Don, 101

C

Calloway, Jim, 137
Carter Law Firm, 3
cases, legal, blogging about, 148–149
Chambers, Paul, 120
Chiffons, The, 43
click tracking, 162
clients
    blogging about, 148–149
    testimonials rule, 150–152
collective works, 56
comments, 65–69
    allowing, 65
    benefits of, 66–67
    editing, 67
    interactive nature of, 143–144
    legal advice requests, 149–150
    legal risks of, 67–69
    moderating, 51, 67–68
    responding to, 66, 163–164
    terms of service and, 108–109
commerce, trademark use, 96–97
commercialization invasions of privacy,
    91–92
commercial purpose
    licensing images for, 30–31
    licensing original content for, 29–30
commercial speech, 142–143
commissioned works, categories of, 55
committing to blogging, 136–137
Communications Decency Act
    defamatory statements and, 76–77
    Section 230, 67, 70
company blogs, guidelines for, 112
confidential information, blogging about,
    148–149
confidential relationships, legal protection
    of, 87
confidential sources, 61–64
Constitutional Daily blog, 6
content
    fair use, 25–30

licensing, 58–59
    from marketing companies, 71
    ownership of, 53–58
    protection from copying, 52
    quality content, 129, 137
    removal or blocking of, 48–49
contract employees, firing of, 111–112
contracts
    copyright ownership and, 55–56
    for copyright transfer, 21–22
    for guest bloggers, 51, 70–71
    oral contracts with information
        sources, 62, 64
    with users of site, 108
    work-made-for-hire contracts,
        53–54, 69–70
controversial blog posts, 164–165, 170
controversial speech, First Amendment
    protections, 8
conversations with readers, 135
copying original works, 44–45
    fair use doctrine and, 25–30
    transformative use, 28
copyrightable works, 15–16
Copyright Act, 15–16
    Digital Millennium Copyright Act
        (DMCA), 45–48
    fair use of others' content, 25–30
    protection for works after creation,
        15–17, 33
    publication, definition of, 37
    registration time frame, 36–37
    works made for hire, 53–54
copyright infringement, 19
    actual damages, 37–38
    copyright registration and, 36–37
    defending against, 29
    de minimus amounts, 39
    detecting, 44–45
    DMCA agents, registering, 50–51
    DMCA takedown notices, 45–48
    fair use doctrine and, 25–30
    federal jurisdiction, 107
    indemnity against, 57
    informing the infringer, 48–49
    lawyers' fees, 38
    remedies, 38
    responding to claims, 72
    safe harbor against, 45–48

statutory damages, 38
unintentional infringement, 43
willful infringement, 38
copyright laws
automatic copyright protection, 18
derivative works, 17–18
expression, protection of, 19–20
public domain, 23–24
rights under, 16–17
transferring copyrights, 21–23
copyright protection, 16–17, 33
giving, selling, or licensing copyrights, 16
of original works of authorship, 15–16
registration with U.S. Copyright Office, 16, 33–41
copyright registration, 16, 33–41
blogs, registering, 33–34, 37–41
derivative works, 36
publication date, 36–37
serial works, 35
copyrights
duration of, 22, 41
for guest posts, 69, 71
inheritance of, 22–23
licensing for use, 30–31
protecting, 43–52
releasing to public domain, 23–24
selling, 59
for single works, 34
transferring, 21–23
copyright trolls, 28–29
Copyscape, 44
Cox, Crystal, 107–108
Creative Commons, 30–31
licensing blogs, 40
credibility, building via blogging, 130–132
crimes
committed via blogging, 119–123
jurisdiction, 127–128. *See also* jurisdiction
punishable by death, 125–127
solicitation of, 122–123
cyberharassment, cyberbullying, and cyberstalking, 121–122
laws listed by state, 177–198

D

damage, reputational, 75–86, 88, 108
damages
actual damages, 37–38
in copyright infringement cases, 36–39
in defamation lawsuits, 79, 81–82
paying, 57, 71
statutory damages, 36–39, 72
death by blogging, 125–128
death sentence, crimes punishable by, 125–127
death threats, 120
Dees, William, 27
defamation, 75–86
actual malice, 80, 82
anonymous persons and, 78–79
damages, 79, 81–82
defenses against, 82–85
definition of, 75
false light claims and, 89–90
indemnifying against claims, 70
liability for, 78
libel, 76
opinions vs. facts, 77–78
of public vs. private persons, 80–82
reckless disregard of the truth, 80–81, 89
responding to claims, 79
slander, 76
true vs. false statements, 83–84
word choice, 76
defenses
against defamation, 82–85
fair use doctrine, 25
derivative works, 16–18
blogs as, 36
Digital Millennium Copyright Act (DMCA), 45–48
abuse of, 51–52
Digital Millennium Copyright Act (DMCA) agents, 45–46
email address for, 72
registering, 50–51, 72–73
Digital Millennium Copyright Act (DMCA) counter notifications, 49–50

Digital Millennium Copyright Act
(DMCA) takedown notices, 45–48
content removal, 48–49
responding to, 49, 68, 72–73
disciplinary action
because of blogging, 111, 117
for employment contract violations,
116–117
disclaimers, 145–147
advertising disclaimers, 143, 145
standard disclaimers, 145–146
disclosure of relationships, 150–154
failure to disclose, 153–154
DOC Cop, 44
drugs, selling online, 122

E

economic motivations for blogs, 143
editorial calendars, 137, 159, 161
Electronic Frontier Foundation, 12
electronic newsletters, 163
e-mail
addresses of DMCA agents, 46, 72
for anonymous blogging, 7
bullying and harassment by, 121–122
interviewing guests by, 73
sharing blog posts by, 163
emotional distress, intentional infliction
of, 87, 92–93
employees
as bloggers, 54–55, 57–58
disciplinary actions against, 111,
116–117
employment contract violations,
116–117
factors in determining employee
status, 57–58
National Labor Relations Act and,
112–114
online behavior, allowable, 111–118
protected concerted activity, 113–115
termination because of blogging,
111–118
employers
assigning copyright to, 56–57
complaints against, 114, 118

compliance with National Labor
Relations Act, 113
copyright ownership, 54–55
indemnity against infringement
claims, 57
social media policies, 117
endorsements and testimonials rules,
150–154
ethical issues, 141–155
advice requests, responding to,
149–150
blogging about cases, 148–149
blog promotion, 157–158
disclaimers and, 145–147
disclosure of relationships, 150–154
paid links, 152–153
recommendations, 152
rules for legal advertising, listed by
state, 177–198
testimonials, 152
expectation of privacy, 87
intrusion into seclusion and, 90–91
expertise, demonstrating via blogging,
130–132

F

Facebook
death threats on, 120
posting about wages and work
conditions on, 113–115
privacy settings, 117
reaching readers on, 162
facts
copyright protection and, 19–20
vs. opinions, 11–12, 77–78
original arrangements of, 20
fair use doctrine, 25–30
commercial use, 29–30
copying the work, 26
effect on potential market, 27
factors of, 26–27
as infringement defense, 28–29
parodies and, 27–28
fake name generators, 7
false light invasions of privacy, 88–90
false statements, 75. See also defamation
federal laws, 199

anti-SLAPP law, 12
jurisdiction and, 106–107
Federal Trade Commission endorsements
  and testimonials rule, 150–154
*Feist Publications, Inc. v. Rural Telephone
  Service Co.*, 19–20, 44
fighting words, 8
First Amendment
  anonymous speech protection, 6–7
  anti-SLAPP laws, 12
  blogging and, 5–13
  defamatory speech and, 75
  expressions about presidential
    administration, 121
  limits to protections, 8–10
  non-protected speech, 8
fixed tangible mediums, 15
flash mob law, 130
freedom of speech, 5–6
free information via blogs, 137–138
free merchandise, disclosure of
  relationships and, 150–154

G

geographic location
  disguising, 7
  of injury occurrence, 107
  personal jurisdiction and, 105–106
  for trademark use, 96–98
getting arrested because of blogging,
  119–123
getting fired because of blogging,
  111–118
  National Labor Relations Act and,
    112–114
Ghonim, Wael, 7
giving it away for free, 137–138
goo.gl, 162
Google+, reaching readers on, 162
Google Adwords, 160
Google Images, 44
griping vs. protected concerted activity,
  113–114
guest blogging, 166
  alternative to, 73
  contracts for, 71
  exclusive rights to, 71

indemnification for, 70–71
legal risks of, 69–73
licensing of, 71
work-made-for-hire contracts, 69–70
Gwire, William, 77–78

H

harassment laws, 121–122
Harrison, George, 43
Help A Reporter Out (HARO),
  131–132
hidden cameras, microphones, and/or
  transmitters, obtaining information
  via, 90–91
Hilton, Perez, 20
hosting companies, copyright
  infringement protection, 45, 47
human body parts, selling online, 122
Hunter v. Virginia State Bar, 142–143

I

ideas, copyright protection and, 19
identity of information sources,
  protecting, 61–64
illegal sales, 122
illegal speech, 119–123
images
  with blog posts, 136
  commercialization of, 91–92
  licensing for use, 30–31
  permission for use, 31
  searching for, 44
implied licenses, 56
indemnification
  against copyright infringement
    claims, 51, 57, 68
  for guest posts, 70–71
independent contractors
  as bloggers, 55–58
  employment status, 57–58
  works made for hire by, 55–56
individuals. *See also* private persons
  building relationships with, 67
  defamation of, 75
  First Amendment protections, 12
  invasions of privacy, 88

threats against, 9
inflammatory speech, First Amendment
    protections, 8
information sources, protecting identity
    of, 61–64
Inman, Matt, 18
intellectual property rights
    of guest posts, 70
    indemnifying against violation claims,
        70
intentional infliction of emotional
    distress, 92–93
    state laws on, 87
international blog posts, jurisdiction and,
    109
international laws on crimes punishable
    by death, 125–127
interviews, 73
intestacy laws, copyrights and, 22–23
intrusion into seclusion invasions of
    privacy, 90–91
invasions of privacy, 88
    false light invasions, 88–90
    indemnifying against claims, 70
    intrusion into seclusion invasions,
        90–91
    misappropriation or
        commercialization invasions,
        91–92
    public disclosure of private facts
        invasions, 90
    state laws, 87
IP addresses, identity tracing through, 7
IP-Lookup.net, 46

J

jesting statements, 116
jokes, 116
journalists
    bloggers as, 62, 64
    shield laws for, 61–64
journalist's motto, 2
jurisdiction, 105–109
    over blog content, 127–128
    personal jurisdiction, 105–106
    state laws and, 106–109
    subject matter jurisdiction, 105–107

terms of service, establishing with,
    108–109

K

keywords, 160–161
knowledge, demonstrating via blogging,
    130–132

L

Las Vegas Review Journal, 28–29
Lavandeira, Mario, 20
law firm blogs, 53
lawyer-client privilege, 91
    disclosing information publically, 10
lawyer's fees
    for copyright infringement, 38
    resolution of, 68–71
legal advice requests, 149–150
legal cases, blogging about, 148–149
legal side of blogging
    federal laws, 12, 199
    state laws, listed by state, 177–198.
        See also state laws
    staying informed, 169
libel, 76
libel-proof plaintiff doctrine, 85
licensing
    content, 58–59
    exclusive licenses, 59
    guest posts, 69–71
    images, 30–31
    implied licenses, 56
    non-exclusive licenses, 59
    to others, 58–59
    search engine optimization and, 58
licensing agreements
    length of license, 59
    limits on use of content, 59
    sublicensing content, 59
limitations on speech, 8–10
LinkedIn
    maximizing account effectiveness,
        162–163
    recommendations, rules on, 152
link shorteners, 162
Lucas, George, 17

M

malice, 80, 82, 84–85, 89, 93
marketing companies, contracting for
content from, 71
Mayer, Eric, 134, 146
McCauley, James, 144
Meier, Megan, 121
Mine, Alicia Neece, 144
misappropriation or commercialization
invasions of privacy, 91–92
Model Rules of Professional Conduct on
advertising and solicitation, 142–144
moderating comments, 67–68
Moriarty, Jeff, 136
Mubarak, Hosni, 7

N

Namby Pamby, The, 6, 173–176
Namby Pamby blog, 6
name-calling, 115
National Labor Relations Act (NLRA),
112–114
gray areas, 117–118
online protected behaviors, 115–116
National Labor Relations Board (NLRB),
112
Nelson, Michael, 28–29
networking
connecting through writing, 135, 138
driving traffic to blog with, 165–166
in real world, 166–167
news information vs. commercialization
of images, 92
niche area of practice, establishing, 130

O

Oatmeal, The, 18
O'Keefe, Kevin, 132, 136
online behavior
allowable, 111–117
gray areas, 117–118
illegal behavior, 119–123
online communications, permanence of,
3–4
online marketing, blogs as, 129, 138

online resources, blogging-related,
201–202
opinions
about free products and services,
150–152
vs. facts, 11–12, 77–78
oral contracts with confidential sources,
62, 64
Orbison, Roy, 27
original authors
attributions of, 26, 30–31
employers as, 54–55
original works of authorship
categorizing for copyright
registration, 33–34
copying, 25–30, 44–45
copyright protection, 15–16, 18
copyright rights on, 16–17
reproducing, 16
ow.ly, 162
ownership of blog, 2

P

Padrick, Kevin, 107–108
paid links, FTC regulation of, 152–153
personality, sharing via blogging, 133–134
personal jurisdiction, 105–106
Phoenix Real Estate Guy, The, 133
Pinterest
copyright infringement and, 132
reaching readers on, 162
plagiarism
detecting, 44–45
DMCA abuse, 51–52
posts. *See* blog posts
Pottermore, 18
president of the United States, threats
against, 120–121
privacy, 87
expectation of, 87, 90–91
in public places, 87
private facts, public disclosure of, 90
private persons. *See also* individuals
defamation of, 80–82
intentional infliction of emotional
distress claims, 92–93

matters of public concern vs. not of
    public concern, 81
product reviews, relationship disclosure
    and, 150–154
professional interaction through blog
    comments, 67
promotion of blog, 157–167
    action plan for, 159
    audience, communicating with,
        161–163
    audience, interacting with, 163–164
    controversial posts, 164–165
    ethical rules for, 157–158
    guest blogging, 166
    networking for, 165–166
    networking in real world, 166–167
    quality content, 158
    responsiveness to readers, 163–164
    tagging posts, 160–161
property transfers, copyright transfers,
    21–22
protected concerted activity, 113
    determining, 118
    name-calling as, 115
proxy servers, 7
pseudonyms
    defamation claims and, 78–79
    First Amendment protections, 6
    registering copyrights with, 40–41
public, expectation of privacy in, 87–88
publication, legal definition of, 37
public disclosure of private facts invasions
    of privacy, 90
public discourse, 9
public domain, releasing works into,
    23–24
public issues, debate on, 5
public performance of original works, 16
public persons
    defamation of, 80–81
    false light claims, 89
    intentional infliction of emotional
        distress claims, 93
public records as original sources, 83
publishers, state and federal laws for, 10

Q

quality content, 129
    creating, 137, 141
    promotional potential of, 158
quotations of defamatory statements, 83

R

readers
    interacting with, 162–163
    interacting with in real world,
        166–167
    inviting to blog posts, 165
    responsiveness to, 163–164
    sharing of posts, 163
    stimulating, 65
    value, providing to, 163–164
readership, 135
    growing, 157–167
    targeting content to, 3
Real Estate Zebra, 101–102
real-world networking, 166–167
reckless disregard of the truth, 80–81
    in false light invasion of privacy, 89
referral sources, 137–138
relationships
    building via blogging, 66–67,
        134–135
    confidential relationships, 87
    disclosure of, 150–154
    disclosure violations, 153–154
    and real-world interactions, 166–167
reprints, permission for, 16–17
Reprint Writers, 44
reproductions of original works, 16
reputation of blogger
    blogging and, 115
    building via blogging, 131–132, 134,
        171
    content quality and, 137
reputation of persons
    damage to, 75–86, 88, 108
    no damage to, 85
requests for advice, responding to,
    149–150
resources, blogging-related, 201–202
revenue, blogging and, 132

reviews of services, relationship disclosure and, 150–154
Righthaven, 28–29
Rothamel, Daniel, 101–102
Rowling, J.K., 17–18
rules on advertising and solicitation, 141–145
Rural Telephone Service, 19–20, 44

S

safe harbor against copyright infringement, 45–48
sales, leasing, and lending of original works, 16
schedule for writing and posting, 136–137
Scholastic, 18
search engine optimization (SEO), 136
   licensed content and, 58
   regular blogging and, 137
   tagging posts, 160–161
search terms, tagging posts with, 160–161
serial works, 35
service marks, 95–96
sex, selling online, 122
sharing blog posts, 163
shield laws, 61–62
   for blogger protection, 63
   listed by state, 177–198
   state differences in, 108
Silver, Elizabeth, 20
Silver v. Lavandeira, 20
slander, 76
Snell and Wilmer website, 146–147
social media
   books on, 203–204
   company policies on, 117
   cyberharassment on, 121–122
   death threats on, 120
   driving traffic to blog with, 161–162
   legal posts, 123
   marketing best practices, keeping up with, 169
   marketing on, 129
   networking on, 165–166
   privacy settings, 117
   reaching readers with, 162

sharing posts on, 163
social media accounts
   ownership of, 54–55
   promotion through, 55
solicitation, 122–123
   avoiding, 144–145
   definition of, 144
   rules on, 141–145
sources
   finding, 132
   protecting identity of, 61–64
speaking the truth, 1–2
Star Wars movies, 17
state laws
   on advertising and solicitation, 141
   on assault, 119–120
   blogging-related laws, listed by state, 177–198
   on cyberharassment, 121–122, 177–198
   jurisdiction and, 106–109
   shield laws, 61–63, 108, 177–198
   solicitation laws, 122–123
statements of fact vs. opinion, 11–12
stolen property, selling online, 122
storytelling via blogging, 135
strategic lawsuits against public participation (SLAPP)
   anti-SLAPP laws, 177–198
subject matter jurisdiction, 105–107
subscription options for blogs, 163
Svenson, Ernie, 138
swear words, 9

T

tagging blog posts with keywords, 160–161
takedown notices, 45–49
   responding to, 49, 68, 72–73
   validity of, 47–48
tangible mediums, 15
target audience, 135. *See also* readers; readership
   reaching, 161–163
termination of employment because of blogging, 111–118
terms of service, 68–69, 72

dispute resolution clause, 68–69
infringing material removal clause, 73
jurisdiction, establishing with,
108–109
Terra, Evo, 170
testimonials rules, 150–154
text messages, cyberharassment by,
121–122
thick skin for blogging, 170
Thompson, Jay, 133
threats, 9
against U.S. president, 120–121
of violence, 8, 116, 119–120
topics to write about, 137
choosing, 150
tracking clicks, 162
trademark infringement, 98, 100–103
jurisdiction over, 107
protecting against, 103
trademark law, 95–103
blogs, problems related to, 100–103
geographic markets, 96–98
listed by state, 177–198
registering trademarks, 96–97,
99–100, 102–103
service marks, defined, 95–96
TM and registered symbols, 99
trademark protection, 96–99
trademark searches, 98–99
trademarks, 95–96
abandoned, 100
affidavits of use, 100
traffic
driving to blog, 161–162
from networking with professionals,
165–166
tracking clicks, 162
transfer of copyright, 21–23
contracts, recording, 22
disputes about, 22
exclusive vs. nonexclusive rights, 21
purchasing rights back, 22
state laws on, 21
trouble, avoiding, 4
true threats, 9
truth
impact of, 1–2
publishing, 93

reckless disregard of, 80–81, 89
in reviews and endorsements,
151–152, 154
Twitter
death threats on, 120
privacy settings, 117
2 Live Crew, 27–28

U

Undeniable Ruth, The, blog, 2, 136
Unwashed Advocate blog, 134, 146
U.S. Constitution copyright authority, 15
U.S. Copyright Office
anonymous blogs, registering with,
40–41
blogs, registering with, 33–41
copyright records, transferring, 22
registration, cost-effectiveness of, 39
works, registering with, 16
U.S. Patent and Trademark Office
(USPTO)
Intent To Use applications, 96–97
trademarks, registering with, 96–99
U.S. president, threats against, 120–121

V

Vaynerchuk, Gary, 131, 135
verbal attacks, 8
verbal speech, freedom of, 6
violence, threats of, 119–120
visual images from Creative Commons,
30–31

W

wages
employee-employer discussions on,
112–114
posting about, 114–115
Walt Disney Company, 17
Warner Brothers, 17–18
website analytics
click tracking, 162
copyright infringement, detecting
through, 45
website hosting companies

copyright infringement protection, 45, 47

DMCA takedown notices, 46–48

websites

blog subscription options, 163

linking to informational sites, 163–164

static nature of, 130–131

terms of service, 68–69, 72–73, 108–109

WhoIs.com, 46

willful infringement, 38

Williams, Katt, 170

wills, residuary clauses, 22–23

Wilson, Julia, 120–121

word choice

defamation and, 76

facts, distinguishing from opinions, 11–12

WordPress social media plug-in, 163

work conditions

employee-employer discussions, 112–114

posting about, 114–115

workplace, intrusion into seclusion claims in, 91

works made for hire, 53–54

contracts for, 69–70

employee blog posts, 54–55

by independent contractors, 55–56

licensing for limited use, 59

writing. *See also* blogging

schedule for, 136–137, 159

speaking the truth, 1–2

topics, choosing, 150

writs of mandamus, 79

written speech, freedom of, 6

Y

Yelp, 77

YouTube, copyright infringement protection, 45

Z

Zebra Report and *Zebra Blog,* 101–102

Zillow, 133

How to Start and Build a Law Practice, 5th Ed
By Jay G. Foonberg

Product Code: 5110508 • **LP Price:** $57.95 • **Regular Price:** $69.95

If you have a question about starting and growing your own law practice, or improving your existing solo or small firm practice, Jay Foonberg has the answers in this power-packed, updated, and expanded new edition. Learn it all from a practicing lawyer who provides you with real answers, for real practices, gained from real experiences.

This classic ABA bestseller has been used by tens of thousands of lawyers as the comprehensive guide to planning, launching, and growing a successful practice. It's packed with over 600 pages of guidance on identifying the right location, finding clients, setting fees, managing your office, maintaining an ethical and responsible practice, maximizing available resources, upholding your standards, and much more. If you're committed to starting your own practice, this book will give you the expert advice you need to make it succeed.

The Lawyer's Essential Guide to Writing
By Marie Buckley

Product Code: 5110726 • **LP Price:** $47.95 • **Regular Price:** $79.95

This is a readable, concrete guide to contemporary legal writing. Based on Marie Buckley's years of experience coaching lawyers, this book provides a systematic approach to all forms of written communication, from memoranda and briefs to e-mail and blogs. The book sets forth three principles for powerful writing and shows how to apply those principles to develop a clean and confident style.

LinkedIn in One Hour for Lawyers, 2nd Ed.
By Dennis Kennedy and Allison C. Shields

Product Code: 5110773 • **LP Price:** $39.95 • **Regular Price:** $49.95

Since the first edition of LinkedIn in One Hour for Lawyers was published, LinkedIn has added almost 100 million users, and more and more lawyers are using the platform on a regular basis. Now, this bestselling ABA book has been fully revised and updated to reflect significant changes to LinkedIn's layout and functionality made through 2013. LinkedIn in One Hour for Lawyers, Second Edition, will help lawyers make the most of their online professional networking. In just one hour, you will learn to:

- Set up a LinkedIn® account
- Create a robust, dynamic profile--and take advantage of new multimedia options
- Build your connections
- Enhance your Company Page with new functionality
- Use search tools to enhance your network
- Monitor your network with ease
- Optimize your settings for privacy concerns
- Use LinkedIn® effectively in the hiring process
- Develop a LinkedIn strategy to grow your legal network

The Legal Career Guide, 5th Edition
By Gary A. Munneke, Ellen Wayne

Product Code: 5110667 • **LP Price:** $34.95 • **Regular Price:** $54.95

With a few simple steps, lawyers can use Facebook® to market their services, grow their practices, and expand their legal network—all by using the same methods they already use to communicate with friends and family. *Facebook® in One Hour for Lawyers* will show any attorney—from Facebook® novices to advanced users—how to use this powerful tool for both professional and personal purposes.

Job Quest for Lawyers: The Essential Guide to Finding and Landing the Job You Want
By Sheila Nielsen

Product Code: 5110725 • **LP Price:** $39.95 • **Regular Price:** $49.95

Job Quest for Lawyers provides step-by-step guidance that finally makes networking inspiring instead of a chore. The "quest" motif applies to each stage of the job search, and is used to help readers understand how to create a positive and effective networking experience. The book demystifies networking by including illustrations from the author's own experiences and from the stories of her clients that provide examples of the real world do's and don'ts of how to conduct a productive job search. Unlike so many other career books, Job Quest for Lawyers is a process-focused book that is eminently applicable to attorneys at all phases of their careers, from new graduates to senior lawyers. Lawyers at all stages of practice will benefit from reading this book.

Entertainment Careers for Lawyers, 3rd Ed.
By William D. Henslee

Product Code: 5110769 • **LP Price:** $32.95 • **Regular Price:** $54.95

Entertainment Careers for Lawyers, Third Edition, will dispel many of the myths surrounding the practice and help lawyers and law students gain an understanding of the realities of entertainment law. Written by William D. Henslee, an experienced entertainment lawyer and law professor, this book will help you gain an overview of the substantive law areas included in entertainment law, from intellectual property and litigation to contract negotiations and estate planning. You will also earn about the career trajectories available in four major entertainment genres: music, theater, film, and television.

Nonlegal Careers for Lawyers, Fifth Edition
By William D. Henslee, Gary A. Munneke, Ellen Wayne

Product Code: 5110567 • **LP Price:** $29.95 • **Regular Price:** $34.95

Perhaps you are a law student who realizes that practicing law is not what you want to do. Or maybe you are a practicing lawyer who no longer feels satisfied with your work. If you feel it's time for a change, this newly revised guidebook will show you what you can do with your law degree, besides practice law. More importantly, this book will illustrate how to use your legal skills to rise above the competition.

iPad in One Hour for Lawyers, Second Edition
By Tom Mighell

Product Code: 5110747 • LP Price: $24.95 • Regular Price: $39.95

Whether you are a new or a more advanced iPad user, *iPad in One Hour for Lawyers* takes a great deal of the mystery and confusion out of using your iPad. Ideal for lawyers who want to get up to speed swiftly, this book presents the essentials so you don't get bogged down in technical jargon and extraneous features and apps. In just six, short lessons, you'll learn how to:

- Quickly Navigate and Use the iPad User Interface
- Set Up Mail, Calendar, and Contacts
- Create and Use Folders to Multitask and Manage Apps
- Add Files to Your iPad, and Sync Them
- View and Manage Pleadings, Case Law, Contracts, and other Legal Documents
- Use Your iPad to Take Notes and Create Documents
- Use Legal-Specific Apps at Trial or in Doing Research

Personal Branding In One Hour for Lawyers
By Katy Goshtasbi

Product Code: 5110765 • LP Price: $39.95 • Regular Price: $49.95

With over 1.2 million licensed attorneys in the United States, how do lawyers stand out from their fellow practitioners and get jobs, promotions, clients, and referrals? To survive and thrive, lawyers must develop their own intentional personal brand to distinguish themselves from the competition. In Personal Branding in One Hour for Lawyers, personal branding expert and experienced attorney Katy Goshtasbi explains how attorneys can highlight their unique talents and abilities, manage their perceptions, and achieve greater success as a lawyer in the process. In just one hour, you will learn to:

- Discover your personal brand--and why it matters to colleagues and clients
- Use your personal brand as a marketing tool
- Stand out from the crowd--improve your visual brand by making simple, yet impactful, changes to your attire and personal appearance
- Create effective marketing materials for your brand
- Network successfully to implement your personal brand
- Communicate your brand effectively

The Lawyer's Guide to Professional Coaching
By Andrew Elowitt

Product Code: 5110735 • LP Price: $47.95 • Regular Price: $79.95

Become more efficient and profitable in your law practice by employing a professional coach. The Lawyer's Guide to Professional Coaching will teach you to find, select, and work productively with the right coach for your needs--and transform your practice in the process. Learn how to get the most out of coaching, decide whether coaching is right for you and your firm, and use coaching skills when you manage, mentor, and collaborate with client and colleagues.

Lessons in Leadership: Essential Skills for Lawyers
By Thomas C. Grella

Product Code: 5110761 • LP Price: $47.95 • Regular Price: $79.95

More lawyers than ever before are using Twitter to network with colleagues, attract clients, market their law firms, and even read the news. But to the uninitiated, Twitter's short messages, or tweets, can seem like they are written in a foreign language. Twitter in One Hour for Lawyers will demystify one of the most important social-media platforms of our time and teach you to tweet like an expert. In just one hour, you will learn to:

- Create a Twitter account and set up your profile
- Read tweets and understand Twitter jargon
- Write tweets—and send them at the appropriate time
- Gain an audience—follow and be followed
- Engage with other Twitters users
- Integrate Twitter into your firm's marketing plan
- Cross-post your tweets with other social media platforms like Facebook and LinkedIn
- Understand the relevant ethics, privacy, and security concerns
- Get the greatest possible return on your Twitter investment

Virtual Law Practice: How to Deliver Legal Services Online
By Stephanie L. Kimbro

Product Code: 5110707 • LP Price: $47.95 • Regular Price: $79.95

The legal market has recently experienced a dramatic shift as lawyers seek out alternative methods of practicing law and providing more affordable legal services. Virtual law practice is revolutionizing the way the public receives legal services and how legal professionals work with clients. If you are interested in this form of practicing law, *Virtual Law Practice* will help you:

- Responsibly deliver legal services online to your clients
- Successfully set up and operate a virtual law office
- Establish a virtual law practice online through a secure, client-specific portal
- Manage and market your virtual law practice
- Understand state ethics and advisory opinions
- Find more flexibility and work/life balance in the legal profession

The Lawyer's Essential Guide to Writing
By Marie Buckley

Product Code: 5110726 • LP Price: $47.95 • Regular Price: $79.95

This is a readable, concrete guide to contemporary legal writing. Based on Marie Buckley's years of experience coaching lawyers, this book provides a systematic approach to all forms of written communication, from memoranda and briefs to e-mail and blogs. The book sets forth three principles for powerful writing and shows how to apply those principles to develop a clean and confident style.

30-DAY RISK-FREE ORDER FORM

Please print or type. To ship UPS, we must have your street address. If you list a P.O. Box, we will ship by U.S. Mail.

Name

Member ID

Firm/Organization

Street Address

City/State/Zip

Area Code/Phone (In case we have a question about your order)

E-mail

Method of Payment:

☐ Check enclosed, payable to American Bar Association
☐ MasterCard ☐ Visa ☐ American Express

Card Number   Expiration Date

Signature Required

MAIL THIS FORM TO:
American Bar Association, Publication Orders
P.O. Box 10892, Chicago, IL 60610

ORDER BY PHONE:
24 hours a day, 7 days a week:
Call 1-800-285-2221 to place a credit card order. We accept Visa, MasterCard, and American Express.

EMAIL ORDERS: orders@americanbar.org
FAX ORDERS: 1-312-988-5568

VISIT OUR WEB SITE: www.ShopABA.org
Allow 7-10 days for regular UPS delivery. Need it sooner? Ask about our overnight delivery options. Call the ABA Service Center at 1-800-285-2221 for more information.

GUARANTEE:
If—for any reason—you are not satisfied with your purchase, you may return it within 30 days of receipt for a refund of the price of the book(s). No questions asked.

Thank You For Your Order.

Join the ABA Law Practice Division today and receive a substantial discount on Division publications!

Product Code:	Description:	Quantity:	Price:	Total Price:
				$
				$
				$
				$
				$

Shipping/Handling:		*Tax:	Subtotal:	$
$0.00 to $9.99	add $0.00	IL residents add 9.25% DC residents add 5.75%	*Tax:	$
$10.00 to $49.99	add $6.95			
$50.00 to $99.99	add $8.95		**Shipping/Handling:	$
$100.00 to $199.99	add $10.95	Yes, I am an ABA member and would like to join the Law Practice Division today! (Add $50.00)	$
$200.00 to $499.99	add $13.95		Total:	$